CONSUMER GUIDE®

COMPACT DISC PLAYERS
BUYING GUIDE

CONTENTS

CHAPTER 1

Introducing the Digital Disc

Most people have been listening to recorded music in essentially the same way for nearly 110 years. The modern LP (long-playing) record stores music in the form of "wiggles," or jagged surfaces, in a groove. (While it appears that there are numerous grooves in a record, there is actually only one continuous groove.) The wiggles correspond to the sound waves that are picked up by microphones at the time of the live musical performance. The electrical signals from those microphones are amplified until they are powerful enough to drive a cutting stylus, or needle. This stylus cuts the groove and its wiggles in a "master disc," which is used to produce the vinyl LP record that you play on your phonograph.

In the late 1870s, Thomas Edison spoke those immortal words, "Mary had a little lamb,..." into a large inverted horn that was attached to a diaphragm and cutting stylus, which vibrated in accordance with the sound waves produced by Edison's voice. The vibrating stylus scratched a continuous groove with "hill-and-dale" (up and down) wiggles on the surface of a tinfoil-wrapped cylinder. (Later on, these vertical wiggles were replaced by the horizontal ones used on today's albums.) The sound of Edison's invention was crude compared with that of a modern LP record played on a High-Fidelity audio system, but the principles of recording and playback were the same.

By the mid-1920s, the mechanical horn had given way to microphones, and electrical recording replaced the mechanical method. Shortly after World War II, Peter Goldmark, working at CBS Laboratories, developed the long-playing (LP) record, which replaced the 78 rpm (revolutions per minute), shellac-based records of that era. The grooves in vinyl LP records were much narrower than those in 78 rpm albums, and the LPs played for more than 20 minutes per side.

The post-war era also witnessed the development of the audiotape recorder. Professional tape recorders enabled recording companies to store and edit musical performances on magnetic tape before transferring the signals to a master LP disc. The tape recorder freed the performer from having to record an entire selection, from start to finish, in one continuous "take." Furthermore, multitrack tape recorders, which record each microphone's output on a separate magnetic track, allowed record producers to remix and rebalance those tracks to produce the desired sound.

When stereophonic records came along in the late 1950s, a sense of spatial realism was added to recorded music. This let you determine the approximate points from which specific instrumental and vocal sounds were coming. Two loudspeakers reproduced left- and right-channel sounds to create a broad "soundstage" in front of you. As for the stereo records, there was one pattern of wiggles on one wall (side) of the groove, and a different wiggle pattern on the opposite groove wall. Yet, with all of the improvements made in recording technology since Edison's time, the basic principle of recording and reproducing sound had not changed; the sound was still represented by wiggles in a record's groove.

ANALOG VERSUS DIGITAL RECORDING

All of the above recording methods employ a system called *analog recording*. The groove in the record is analogous to the sound wave pattern that it is supposed to represent. When sounds are louder, the depth of the groove increases. A low-frequency, bass tone causes the wiggles, or undulations, to occur at a slower rate, while a high-pitched, treble tone is represented by a greater number of wiggles over a given length of the record's groove.

In fact, an analog record groove really has only two characteristics: amplitude and frequency. These continuously varying characteristics are sufficient to define and store the complex sound patterns that we call music. When you stop to think about it, the fidelity of a modern LP record is truly amazing. Nearly all of the frequencies, or tones, that a human being is able to hear can be stored in the groove of an LP record. Given a high-quality turntable and phonograph cartridge, along with a good set of stereophonic audio components, music reproduced from an LP record can be quite satisfying.

Still, even the best LP record has several disadvantages. For one thing, it is subject to wear. No matter how carefully you handle records, the needle, or stylus, will eventually wear away the more delicate groove undulations; many of us are not all that careful. Let the tonearm accidentally drop on a record, and the stylus will probably slide across the record, producing a long, visible scratch. The next time you play that damaged record, you will hear an annoying click, or pop, every time the stylus passes over that scratch. Even if your records have no scratches, when played at loud volumes, you will probably notice that during quieter musical passages, you can hear that ever-present background noise, or hiss, that's called record surface noise.

Another common defect often observed when playing LP records is called *wow-and-flutter*. Its audible effect is a constant wavering of pitch, occurring either once every record revolution, or at a more rapid or fluttering rate. Wow-and-flutter is caused by variations in the speed of the turntable. While better, more expensive turntables have managed to reduce wow-and-flutter effects to inaudible levels, the record itself can cause wow-and-flutter if its center hole is not perfectly concentric with (having the same center point, or curving in an identical manner as) the record grooves themselves.

Finally, as far as musical realism is concerned, the LP record, as good as it is today, still cannot handle the true *dynamic range* of music. Dynamic range, simply put, is the difference between the loudest and softest sounds in any musical selection. The loudest parts of a live musical performance may be 70 or 75 *decibels* (dB) louder than the softest passages of that same selection. One decibel is generally regarded as the smallest change in volume that the average listener can detect. An increase of 10 decibels is perceived by most people as a doubling of the loudness level. Therefore, a dynamic range of 70 dB would amount to an apparent doubling of the sound level seven times. In other words, the loudest sound would seem to be 128 times (seven 2's multiplied together) as loud as the softest sound.

The very best LP records made today can handle only a dynamic range of between 60 and 65 dB. Low-cost records made from less than the finest grade of vinyl barely manage 50 dB of dynamic range. In any analog recording, dynamic range is limited at both extremes of volume (softest and loudest); figure 1–1 shows how dynamic range is limited in an LP record.

The lower limitation is the residual noise level of the medium, which in the case of an LP, means the background surface noise of the disc. Sounds that, in the real world, should be recorded at levels lower than that of the disc surface noise will be buried, or masked, by that surface noise.

The upper limitation of dynamic range in an LP record has to do with the groove wiggles. You'll re-

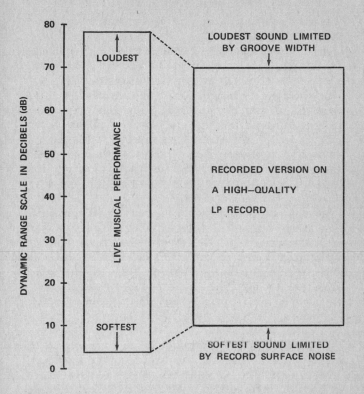

Figure 1–1. The full dynamic range of music cannot "fit" within the limitations of an LP record, so engineers need to compress the music.

member we said that louder sounds require greater amplitude of the wiggles. But if wiggle amplitude is too great, the cutting needle would break through one groove and cut into an adjacent one. One solution would be to space the grooves farther apart, but then the playing time of a record would be drastically reduced. So, given the playing time of a standard LP and its residual surface noise, the best that we can hope for is a dynamic range of around 60 to 65 dB.

In order to "fit" a musical performance into the limited dynamic range of an LP record, a recording engineer has to perform some electronic trickery. The loudest passages of music must be *compressed,* or reduced, so that they aren't quite so loud as to break through the side wall of the record groove. As for the very quiet musical passages, the recording engineer often must boost their loudness level during recording so that they don't get lost beneath the residual surface noise of the final recording.

It is this compression process that results in musical reproduction from LP records that is not truly realistic. Most of us can tell, without entering the room, whether the music is live or recorded. One of the clues we unconsciously use to make that judgment is the presence (or absence) of true, full dynamic range. When we hear music that is compressed, we immediately know that it is not coming from live musicians or vocalists.

In the case of a recording made by a tape recorder, the same situation holds true, except that the lower limitation of dynamic range is tape hiss. This is caused by both the magnetic particles embedded in the tape surface and the electronic circuitry that is used to impart a magnetic pattern to the tape when sounds are recorded. No matter how small the particles or how perfectly they are embedded in the tape, as they pass in front of the tape head during playback, random noise, or hiss, signals are generated. When these signals are amplified, they are heard as tape hiss.

As with LP records, if there are musical signals that are lower in amplitude (loudness level) than that of the tape hiss, the music will be lost, or buried, beneath the noise. At the other end of the scale, if a recording engineer tries to record the loudest portions of a live musical program on tape, the signal will saturate the tape (try to magnetize it beyond its capacity); it's like a sponge that can't hold anymore liquid. The result would be high levels of audible distortion. So, even in the case of audiotape, recording engineers must introduce some compression, reducing the maximum loudness levels and increasing the volume of the very softest musical passages.

Professional tape recorders that are used to make master recordings for subsequent transfer to LP records generally can handle a greater dynamic range than can be accommodated by an LP. However, during the creation of the final two-track stereo version of an album, some of that dynamic range must often be sacrificed. Each step in the process adds some noise to the final tape recording, thereby reducing the total dynamic range of the final master recording.

DIGITAL RECORDING

Let's see how *digital recording*, which is at the heart of the Compact Disc, differs from analog recording. In any digital recording system, it is necessary to look at, or *sample*, the musical *waveform* (the graphic representation that usually shows the sound's amplitude in relation to its frequency) that we want to *digitize* (convert into 1's and 0's that can be processed by computer chips, as exist in CD players). Sampling must be done many times per second; we'll see how many samples are required in a moment.

Suppose the waveform we want to digitize is nothing more than a simple sine wave, as illustrated at the top of figure 1-2. We could measure the amplitude of that waveform at specific intervals, and express those values numerically. Thus, our first sample (actually, sample number 0) would be 8 on a scale of 0 to 15. The next sample (number 1) would be 13, then 15, 13, and so on, until we measure the waveform 8 times, returning to its original amplitude level (8, as in sample number 0) and starting all over again.

Under the samples waveform in figure 1-2, a column of figures is listed in parentheses. These numbers are the familiar *decimal-based numbers* that we use all the time. It is possible, however, to represent these figures using a different numbering system, which is known as the *binary system.* In a binary numbering system, only two digits are used: 0 and 1.

To begin with, the idea of representing analog patterns (in this case, an analog audio signal) with digits is nothing new. The graphics that appear on the screen of a computer or on the video games in your local arcade are generated by numbers, or digits. A computer, in fact, uses a binary numbering system and recognizes these same two digits (0 and 1). These digits are all that's needed to create a complete numbering system. After all, in our daily activities we use a numbering system that contains only ten digits (0 through 9), yet with these few digits we can construct an infinite range of numerical values.

Getting back to the series of numbers under our sine wave in figure 1-2, each of the sample points that we previously expressed as a decimal number has been translated to its equivalent binary number. Thus, the first sample, with a value of 8, is converted to 1000 when expressed in binary notation, while 13, our second sample, becomes 1101, and so on.

Binary numbers are constructed using "powers" of 2. Thus, the digit at the far right in a binary number represents either decimal 0 or decimal 1. The next digit to the left, if it is a 1, adds 2 to the number at the far right; if it is a 0, it adds nothing. Thus, 0010 is equal to decimal 2 (or 2 + 0), while 0011 is equivalent to decimal 3

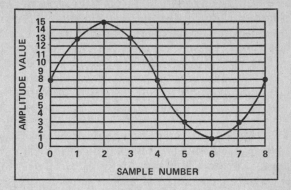

Figure 1-2. To convert an analog signal to a digital signal, the audio waveform (top) is sampled. The numerical sample values are expressed using a binary numbering system (below).

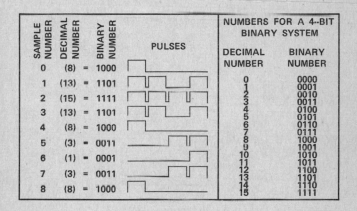

(or 2 + 1). The third digit to the left, if it is a 1, adds decimal 4 to the total, so 0111 would equal decimal 7 (or 4 + 2 + 1). The fourth digit to the left, if it is a 1, represents decimal 8, so the binary number 1111 equals 15 in the decimal system (8 + 4 + 2 + 1).

Introducing the Digital Disc

Once the amplitude samples of our waveform have been expressed as binary numbers, all those digits can be thought of as voltage pulses (1's), or the absence of voltage pulses (0's), as shown in the lower diagram of figure 1-2. Such pulses can, for example, be recorded on tape and, during playback, be reconverted into a continuous waveform by a reverse process known as *digital-to-analog* (D/A) conversion.

In the example shown in figure 1-2, we used only 4 binary digits (or *bits*, as they are called in computer terminology) to represent each sample. Furthermore, we took very few samples—only 8 for the entire duration of the waveform. If we recreated the original waveform using this crude sampling method, the recovered waveform would look like that shown in figure 1-3. Instead of a smooth, continuous sine wave,

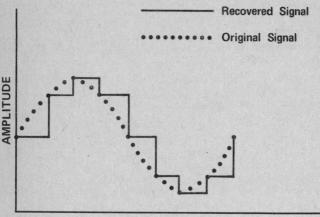

Figure 1-3. If a digital encoding system were limited to a 4-bit code (as illustrated in figure 1-2), and too few samples of the waveform were taken, the decoded (recovered) signal would barely resemble the original, smoothly curving signal.

we would have a highly distorted one with discrete steps. To have the recovered signal look like the original, we must increase the number of bits (binary digits) per sample, and take more samples in a given amount of time.

The first home-audio products to use digital recording techniques were not Compact Disc players; they were *digital-audio processors.* These devices, first sold in 1977, simply converted analog audio signals into a string of binary samples, which could then be recorded on a suitable tape recorder. Each sample contained 14 bits (binary digits), and there were more than 44,000 samples per second! Assuming that 14 bits per sample could mean as many as 14 voltage pulses per sample, and multiplying 14 by 44,000 samples per second, we come up with the staggering number of 616,000 pulses per second. But that's only one channel of information. If you want to record the two channels of a stereo program, you would have to double that number, arriving at 1,232,000 pulses per second!

No ordinary audiotape recorder can handle that many pulses per second; most home audiocassette decks can barely record frequencies up to 20,000 cycles per second (hertz). But even in 1977, there was one kind of tape recorder that could handle such high frequencies (discrete pulses per second). That tape recorder was—as you might've guessed—the home video recorder, which had been introduced two years earlier.

Video signals have very high frequencies—much higher than audio frequencies. Videocassette recorders, or VCRs, use rapidly spinning drums that contain record and playback *tape heads* (electromagnetic pickup devices). Even though the tape moves very slowly, the effective tape-to-tape-head speed in a VCR is about 30 feet per second, as the spinning head drum lays down narrow, diagonal tracks across the width of the slowly moving tape. At that high tape-to-tape-head speed, the high frequencies contained in either video or digital-audio signals can "fit" very nicely on videotape.

While very few home-audio enthusiasts have availed themselves of such digital-audio processors to be used with their videocassette recorders, many professional recording studios and semiprofessional audio experts use such combinations to produce very high quality digital tape recordings.

DIGITAL ADVANTAGES

Consider the advantages of a digital tape recording system, such as the one we have just described. To begin with, tape hiss is no longer a problem. While playing back a digitally recorded tape, the tape head merely has to count pulses, or the absence of pulses. The inherent low-level tape hiss is so low in amplitude that it can never be mistaken for a binary 1 or magnetically recorded pulse. Next, consider the number of bits per sample and what that means in terms of distortion. Since there are 14 bits per sample, there are enough binary numbers to describe 16,384 discrete signal amplitude levels (fourteen 2's multiplied together). Suppose that a given moment in a musical sample has an amplitude that's midway between two available binary numbers; say the value of the sampling is really 16,301.4. The system will have to interpret that level as 16,301. That represents an error (or, a distortion factor) of 0.4 parts in 16,301, or a distortion of only 0.00245%. Analog tape recorders typically deliver distortion levels of 1%, or more, when playing loud passages of music. Therefore, digital distortion is insignificant.

Another advantage of such a digital tape recording scheme occurs when copies are made. So long as you copy such tapes directly (digital code to digital code), there is no deterioration of sound quality with each successive dubbing of the tape. In the case of analog tape recordings, each time you make a duplicate, the copy has more background noise than the original. If you continue the process, the fourth and fifth generation copies are so full of tape hiss and distortion that they are no longer worth listening to. With digital tape recordings, all you are copying is a series of uniform pulses; so long as they are recognizable as such during playback, the music you hear will be as noise-free as the original tape.

Finally, there's the advantage of perfectly flat frequency response. All tones of the original program are reproduced with the correct relative amplitude. Only the very best analog tape recorders can record the full spectrum of audio frequencies from 20 Hz (hertz, or cycles per second) to 20,000 Hz. Yet even the best analog tape recorders have trouble recording the highest frequencies at loud levels.

Not so in the case of a digital tape recording system. The highest frequency that can be perfectly recorded is half the sampling frequency. Since the standard used for digital audiotape recording (using a VCR and digital-audio processor) has been set at over 44,000 samples per second, this means that, in theory, frequencies up to 22,000 Hz can be digitally recorded. In actuality, the system works fine up to 20,000 Hz, which is the accepted limit of human hearing.

Finally, it can be shown that for each bit (binary digit) used for a digital sample, you can expect to realize a dynamic range of approximately 6 decibels (dB). Thus, in a 14-bit digital sampling system, the available dynamic range will be on the order of 84 dB! That's more dynamic range than you will ever encounter in a musical performance. Therefore, at last, there was a medium that could capture the true dynamic range of live music without having to compress it prior to transferring the music to an LP or audiotape.

DEVELOPMENT OF A STANDARD FOR DIGITAL DISCS

Ever since the development of digital-audio processors for digital audiotape recording, many companies tried to come up with an acceptable system for producing digital-audio records, or discs. Three basic approaches were attempted by different Japanese and European companies. Nine companies favored an optical system using a laser beam to "read" encoded 0's and 1's from the surface of a disc. Two companies preferred an electrical type of pickup that would ride on the surface of a grooveless disc. One company endorsed a mechanical system, using discs with grooves and a pickup that "tracks" very lightly.

In June of 1980, the Philips Company of The Netherlands and Sony Corporation of Japan jointly proposed a system that combined Philips' optical (laser beam) pickup technology with Sony's signal-processing technology. Once these two giants of the electronics industry agreed on a single system for digital discs, nearly all other major audio companies quickly agreed to support that system. As a result, you, as a listener, will not have to choose from among several incompatible systems (as with VCRs). There is only one standard for Compact (Digital) Discs, or CDs, as they have become universally known.

The Compact Disc measures only 12 centimeters (about 4¾ inches) in diameter. A single disc, recorded on one side, can play for more than one full hour (theoretically, up to 74 minutes). Digital information is stored beneath the surface of the disc in the form of microscopic depressions, or pits. The pattern of these pits is molded into the disc in a continuous spiral pattern, with a track pitch (distance between circles of pits) that is a mere 1.6 microns wide (a micron is 1 millionth of a meter).

Nothing touches the surface of the disc as it is played. A laser beam impinges (strikes) the pattern of pits, and reflection angles are determined by whether the light strikes a pit or the area where there is no pit (i.e., between pits). These variations in the reflected laser beam represent the 0's and 1's of the digital (binary) code. A photocell converts the light variations into electrical signals, which are amplified and then converted

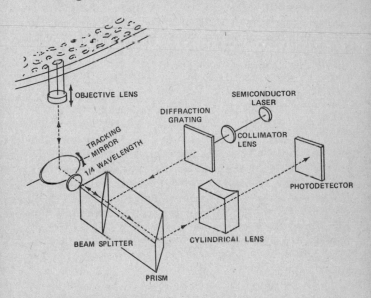

Figure 1-4. Simplified diagram of the optical system used to "read" the digital data in the pits beneath the transparent surface of a Compact Disc.

back into an analog signal before reaching the output jacks of the CD player. One simplified arrangement of this optical system is shown in figure 1-4.

The standards agreed on for the Compact Disc use a sampling rate of 44,100 samples per second; this is not too different from the sampling rate used for digital-audio processors when combined with VCRs. Again, this means perfectly uniform frequency response up to at least 20,000 Hz and down to below the lowest bass tone that humans can hear.

Perhaps more importantly, the number of bits (binary digits) per digital sample was increased from 14 to 16. This means that distortion levels will be even lower. (16-bit samples provide for as many as 65,536 discrete amplitude levels.) As for dynamic range, it is increased to a theoretical maximum of 96 decibels (16 bits multiplied by 6 dB of dynamic range per bit), making this system even more refined than that used in home digital audiotape recording.

MAKING COMPACT DISCS

The process used to produce CDs is far more complex and difficult than that employed for ordinary LPs. Superficially, the steps of each process are remarkably similar. Both LPs and CDs are molded from plastic. But the processes involved in making an acceptable CD are far more costly than those required to make LPs. For one thing, if a microscopic dust particle were to be accidentally molded into a CD, it would ruin the disc. Accordingly, the pressing of CD blanks is done in a sealed "clean room."

There are also many more steps in the production of a CD than there are in making an LP. After molding, the CD must be "vacuum aluminized" so that the laser beam pickup will have a reflective surface to read.

Then, a protective layer of transparent plastic must be applied on top of the aluminized surface containing the actual pits. Final inspection of finished discs involves the use of powerful microscopes, as well as sophisticated computerized checking systems.

It is estimated that the raw cost of a CD, not counting royalties paid to performing artists and the like, is about five times that of a conventional LP. No wonder the price of CDs remains far higher than that charged for ordinary LPs. Currently, CDs cost anywhere from $12 to $16, depending on the content and label (production company). Bear in mind, however, that most CDs offer longer playing times than LPs, which partially compensates for their higher price.

Also contributing to the high price is the fact that there is a world shortage of CDs and CD manufacturing plants. The industry was caught short, never expecting CDs to be accepted so quickly by so many music lovers. CD players have become the fastest growing new technology; three years after their introduction, CD player sales are twice as high as VCRs were at the same point in their history.

So, while CD player prices have come down dramatically since their introduction in early 1983, the cost of the discs have not been reduced to the same extent. As more manufacturing facilities are built and the "yield" of good CDs increases (after production, defective discs are discarded), we may see some price reductions. It is highly unlikely, however, that CDs will ever be as inexpensive as LPs.

CHAPTER 2

Is Your Stereo System "Digital Ready"?

As you begin to shop for a CD player you will probably be told that it can be connected to any existing stereo system. Essentially, that's true, but it doesn't mean that any stereo system will yield the sound quality you expect from your new CD player. Consider the following example:

Suppose you own a receiver or amplifier with a power output rating of 30 watts per channel, and it is hooked up to a pair of medium-efficiency loudspeakers. Until now, you've been playing recordings with the volume control on the receiver set to the loudness level that you like. As far as you've been able to tell, you haven't run into problems of amplifier overload, or distortion, even when loud peaks occur in your favorite records.

You have noticed, however, that if you try to turn the volume up a little more—to loudness levels that are just a bit higher than you like—the amplifier begins to distort; it "runs out of power." Since this occurs only when you turn the volume up beyond the level at which you like to listen, you haven't been too concerned about the problem.

Now, you intend to add a CD player to your system. The salesperson at your favorite audio store tells you that you simply connect the twin cable from the left- and right-channel output jacks of the new CD player to the auxiliary inputs on your receiver, and you'll be all set. If the salesperson is knowledgeable and concerned about how your system will work, you may be asked about the system you already own; in most cases, however, this won't occur. From what we've described up to now, it's clear that your present system was operating at or near its power limits. What will happen when you add a CD player?

First of all, when you adjust the volume control while listening to your CD player, it is likely that you are not going to make it sound any louder than your records or tapes; the average loudness level will be about the same. But recall what we said in Chapter 1 about dynamic range. While the average sound levels may be no different, the occasional peaks that occur in all types of music will now be as much as 10 to 15 decibels louder than they would be if you were playing an ordinary LP record. That's because during the CD recording process, there was no need to compress those peaks. The Compact Disc is able to handle the full dynamic range of music, so the musical peaks come through at full amplitude.

Let's assume that those peaks are only 10 dB greater in amplitude than they would have been on an equivalent LP recording. If your amplifier or receiver was barely adequate for your other program sources, it needs to be able to deliver 10 dB more power when reproducing CDs—at least during peaks in the program material. It may come as a surprise to learn that a 10 dB increase in power represents a 10-to-1 increase in power rating. In other words, all things being equal, if the 30-watts-per-channel amplifier or receiver was barely adequate when playing records or tapes, it must now deliver 300 watts per channel to do the same distortion-free job when reproducing the sounds of Compact Discs.

AUDIO POWER REQUIREMENTS

Before you abandon the idea of owning a CD player, let us reassure you that things are not really quite that bad. For one thing, most of us are not operating our receivers or amplifiers at their maximum limits. In most cases, volume-control levels are set so there is still 4 to 6 dB of margin, or "headroom," before the amplifier begins to distort.

That being the case, the acoustic power increase needed to do justice to CDs is more likely to be between 4 and 6 dB, rather than 10 dB. Fortunately, decibel changes are not linear. A 6 dB change is equal to a power ratio of 4-to-1, while a 3 dB change represents a doubling of power. Even so, it is likely that you are going to need somewhat more acoustic power from your system once you convert to CDs, unless you already have a great deal more power in reserve than you have ever used.

AUDIO-INPUT CIRCUIT REQUIREMENTS

Besides the power output ratings of your receiver or amplifier, you should also look at the specifications for their high-level inputs. CD players deliver output signal voltages of 2 volts or higher; that's considerably more than the output levels you usually get from a tape deck or AM/FM tuner.

Unlike the output signals from your phonograph turntable and cartridge, the cables from a CD player must be connected to a pair of high-level inputs at the back of your amplifier or receiver, not to the "phono" inputs. Suitable high-level inputs will usually be labeled "AUX" or "TUNER." In some cases, the inputs labeled "TAPE" or "TAPE PLAY" are also suitable for connection of a CD player's output cables, if no other high-level inputs are available.

In any case, before connecting your CD player to any pair of inputs, you will want to check out the maximum input level permitted at those inputs before overload or distortion occurs. If this specification is provided, it will look something like this: "Maximum Input Level: Aux, Tuner, or Tape, 5.0 volts; Phono, 200 millivolts (mV)."

As long as the maximum input level is more than 2½ volts or so, you have nothing to worry about. But if the maximum input level rating is less than 2 volts, you will want to choose a CD player that is equipped with an output level control. That way, you can reduce the output level from the CD player so that during recorded peaks, the signal will not overload or exceed the maximum limit of the input stages of the equipment to which it is connected.

LOUDSPEAKER EFFICIENCY

Getting back to power output ratings, we said that when you add a CD player to your system, you are likely to need more acoustic power output than you presently have in your stereo system. There's another way to increase available acoustic power without having to exchange your present amplifier or receiver for a more powerful one; you can switch to a more efficient pair of loudspeaker systems.

Loudspeaker efficiency varies greatly from one design to another. By loudspeaker efficiency we mean the amount of acoustic power you can get from a speaker with a given amount of electrical audio power fed to its terminals. With some loudspeakers, 5 watts of amplifier power applied to their terminals will produce ear-shattering loudness levels. With other speakers, 100 watts of amplifier power may not be enough to create lifelike volume levels. If your present speakers are in the low- or medium-efficiency category, switching to higher efficiency speakers will provide the same increase in available dynamic range as changing to a more powerful amplifier.

Is Your Stereo "Digital Ready"?

How can you tell whether you have a high- or low-efficiency speaker? If the speaker enclosure consists of a small, bookshelf-sized box that is completely sealed, you can be fairly certain it uses a low-efficiency design. Speakers that were favored 10 or 20 years ago generally used a design principle known as acoustic-suspension, or air-suspension. To make these speakers small enough to fit on a bookshelf, designers had to sacrifice efficiency. Speakers such as those made years ago by Acoustic Research (AR), KLH, Advent, and others, were in this category. While their sound quality may have been excellent, they required high-powered amplifiers or receivers to drive them to reasonably loud sound levels.

Speakers that have an opening, or "port," on their front surfaces, or baffles, are generally higher in efficiency than those speakers that employ sealed-box enclosures. Such higher efficiency speakers are usually larger, floor-standing models. Perhaps the most efficient speaker systems are the folded horn-enclosure designs. These are designed to be mounted in two corners of a room, such as the famous Klipsch speakers that have been popular for several decades. Horn-enclosure designs may produce 10 times more acoustic power than bookshelf acoustic-suspension speakers driven from the same amplifier.

SPEAKER EFFICIENCY AND SENSITIVITY

If you have the specification sheet or brochure for your present speakers, you may be able to determine their efficiency from the ratings given in that literature. If you are contemplating the purchase of new speakers to go with your new CD player, the "spec" sheet or brochure describing the speakers you audition will list a specification known as sensitivity. This rating will give you a good idea as to the relative efficiency of the speaker.

The sensitivity of a loudspeaker system is the number of decibels of loudness that the speaker will produce when 1 watt of amplifier power is applied to it, and the measuring microphone or listener is 1 meter in front of the speaker. Typically, low-efficiency speakers, such as the bookshelf types, have sensitivity ratings as low as 80 to 85 dB per watt. Medium-efficiency speakers may have sensitivity ratings between 86 dB and 89 dB per watt, while high-efficiency speakers offer sensitivity ratings higher than 90 dB per watt. The ultra-high efficiency horn enclosures we described earlier can have sensitivity ratings as high as 98 dB, or even higher!

HOW MUCH POWER IS ENOUGH?

Clearly, when you add a CD player to your system, the amount of amplifier (or receiver) power you will need will depend greatly on the type and efficiency of your speakers. Other factors that determine power requirements are the size of your listening room and your personal taste in listening levels. If you always listen to music at very low "background music" loudness levels, you don't have to worry too much about power ratings; a 10- or 20-watt amplifier with low-efficiency speakers will be enough for you. But if like most serious music lovers, you like your music at realistic, lifelike levels, you can use the guidelines in Table 2–1 to determine the approximate amplifier or receiver power that you will need as you convert to CDs and their wider dynamic range.

TABLE 2-1

Amplifier Power vs. Speaker Efficiency

Speaker Sensitivity	Amplifier Power (Watts/Channel) *			
	Listening Preferences			
	Soft	Medium	Loud	Very Loud
80 to 84 dB	20	50	100	200
85 to 89 dB	10	25	50	100
90 to 94 dB	5	15	25	50
Above 94 dB	5	10	20	30

* For small- to average-sized rooms; for much larger rooms, double the above power levels. Also, for systems in which the same amplifier or receiver will be used to power speaker systems in 2 rooms at the same time, double the power levels shown.

"DIGITAL-READY" SPEAKERS

Many speaker manufacturers, aware of the growing popularity of CD players and other digital-audio program sources, have been designing their latest models with digital audio in mind. Generally, that means they have been striving for higher efficiency and greater power handling capability.

Some speaker makers label their newest products as being "Digital Ready." No one has clearly defined just what is meant by that term. Often, it is nothing more than a catchphrase printed on a new tag that is affixed to an old speaker design. In some cases, however, the manufacturer has honestly tried to improve the performance of his products to meet the needs of the new digital-audio age. How can you tell the legitimate "digital-ready" speaker from the other kind? Simply by auditioning the loudspeaker carefully before you spend your money.

Listen to several models of speakers as they reproduce the sounds of CDs. Your audio dealer should have demonstration CDs that tax the capabilities of speakers and amplifiers (or receivers). Such CDs feature extremes of soft and loud passages, fast transients, and sharp musical crescendos, including the sounds made by percussion instruments; in particular, listen to those sharp, loud sounds. Are they clean and crisp, or do they sound muddy and distorted? Does the speaker seem to be "breaking up" those loud sounds? How does the speaker sound when the volume is turned down? (Some speakers sound fine when playing loudly, but tend to produce more distortion when called upon to play at softer levels.)

SPEAKER POWER HANDLING RATINGS

If you decide to keep your present speakers and trade in your amplifier or receiver for a higher powered model as you switch to CDs, make certain your speakers will be able to handle the new, higher power levels produced by your newer audio components. Contrary to popular opinion, speaker systems are not indestructible. If a speaker's maximum power rating is 50 watts, don't expect it to survive for long if it is driven by a 100-watt amplifier operating at, or near, its maximum power ratings. By the same token, if you replace your present speakers for newer, more efficient ones, make certain the new speakers have a maximum power handling capacity that matches your present amplifier or receiver.

Once you've established that your system is ready to accept the signals delivered by a Compact Disc player, you're ready to start shopping for the player itself. In the next chapter we'll talk about all of the features found in CD players—which ones are worth paying extra for, and which ones you will seldom use.

RECORDS AND TAPES ARE NOT OBSOLETE

Many music lovers, having heard about the new CDs and CD players, are asking whether their records and tapes are about to become obsolete. The answer is NO—at least not within the foreseeable future. CDs certainly offer a great many advantages over either records or prerecorded tapes. However, there are currently fewer than 6,000 CD titles available, as compared to 50,000 to 60,000 LP records currently listed in the record catalogs.

Hundreds of millions of turntables exist worldwide, and they are not about to be discarded. It could take five to ten years before the number of CDs purchased equals the number of LP records or prerecorded cassette tapes sold each year. So it is most likely that records and tapes will be around for a long time to come; they will coexist with Compact Discs. And if digital-audio tape (DAT) recorders come along next year or the year after (which seems likely), older analog tape recorders will also coexist with those new digital tape recorder/players.

In other words, a high-quality sound system is a growing entity. As new technology leads to better program sources, such as CDs, those program sources will become another element in your stereo sound system. The moral is: Don't throw out your record player or your tape deck just because you are about to buy a CD player. Continue to enjoy all of your older program sources right along with this latest technological miracle—the Compact Disc.

CHAPTER 3

All CD Players Are Not Created Equal

Since their introduction, several generations of CD players have been designed and produced by the more than three dozen companies that have become licensees of Philips and Sony, the codevelopers of the CD format. Initially, it was thought that all CD players would sound alike. After all, once you are in the "digital domain"—dealing with fixed codes (numbers)—there isn't much room for variation. Every CD player must read the same codes from a given disc.

Audio professionals and consumers soon discovered that there was more to a CD player than just number-code reading circuits. After all, once the number codes have been extracted from the disc, they must be translated back into a familiar analog signal. There are many ways to do this, and not all of them produce equal sonic results. And even if they did, there's the matter of the purely analog amplifier stages that follow the digital-to-analog conversion process. Once the signal is back in the analog domain, there's as much room for variation in sound quality as there is with any other audio component.

Aside from the sound quality differences between players, which are at best rather minimal, there's the matter of convenience and operating features; these differ widely from player to player. Many ingenious operating features found in CD players are a direct result of the foresight of the engineers who created the CD standard in the first place. They incorporated a lot of digital data within the disc format that has nothing to do with the music itself. This "extra" information allows you to extract data concerning the disc's contents and access specific points on the disc in a couple of seconds, or even less. First we'll look at the more obvious external features, and then we'll examine the more subtle internal differences found in today's CD players.

PROGRAMMABILITY: HOW MUCH DO YOU REALLY NEED?

CDs are generally divided into *tracks.* If the Compact Disc contains an album of popular music, each short selection is assigned a different track number. Thus, a CD that offers a dozen songs (some have even more, depending on the length of each song) will have 12 tracks, numbered 1 through 12 on the disc. For classical music, such as a symphony, track numbers are used to separate the piece's movements.

All CD players allow you to call up a specific track number and have the machine begin to play from the start of that track. As you might suspect, some players reach the specified starting point more quickly than others. If you feel that the speed of access is very important, you should test this feature before you decide on a particular CD player. Some machines can even reach any specified point on a disc in one second or less. When you consider the dimensions of the disc and the precision that's required to do this, it is truly remarkable!

A few players let you access a given point on a CD by entering the playing time, as well as the track number. For example, you might tell the player to begin playing at 2 minutes and 38 seconds into track 5. The player's laser pickup assembly, reading the time code that is embedded in the disc's digital code, will then quickly glide to the requested point on the CD and begin to play from that point onward.

The developers of the CD format also provided for additional subdivisions within a given track. For example, a symphonic movement may have more than one melodic theme; such themes may be identified by *index numbers* within a given track. Most of the earliest CD players could not directly access index numbers. Indeed, very few of the early CDs had index points, so there was little need for CD players to be able to access a specific area on a disc by its index number. However, more CDs now utilize this capability, so many of today's CD players let you specify an index point within a given track; once this is done, the laser pickup assembly quickly glides over to that precise point and starts playing there.

The chief difference between CD players that have the lowest price and those that cost a bit more is the latter's programming capabilities. By programming we mean the ability of the machine to store your instructions in its electronic memory and execute them in a given order. A machine without programming memory can play a disc from start to finish, or start to play at a given track, or in some cases, play only one track and then stop.

By contrast, a CD player with programming memory can, at the very least, play specific tracks in ascending sequence (e.g., tracks 1, 4, 7, 9, and 12, in that order). The next level of programming sophistication allows tracks to be played in a random, but specified, fashion (e.g., tracks 5, 2, 4, 3, 9, and so on, in any order you choose). Finally, a few CD players allow you to program tracks and index numbers within a track, in any order you choose.

Not all CD players that offer sophisticated programmability (including random access) provide for the same amount of such programming. Some players can store only six individual programming instructions in memory, while others may accept thirty or more.

All CD Players Are Not Equal

In addition to being able to be programmed to play specific tracks in a given order, many CD players offer a feature called repeat play. If you press a button, these CD players will continue to play a disc until the instruction is canceled. In the case of a machine that has been programmed to play only certain tracks of a disc, pressing the repeat button will cause those tracks to be repeated endlessly.

Taking further advantage of the awesome powers of those miraculous microprocessor chips that are found in CD players (and personal computers), there are even a few players that will randomly shuffle the order of tracks to be played during the repeat-play mode, so that you don't get bored listening to the same selections in the same predictable order, over and over again. You can be sure that the more sophisticated the programming capabilities of a CD player, the more you're going to pay for that machine.

At first glance, programmability seems very desirable, but you should consider just how much programmability you really need and how often you are likely to use such elaborate features. If you usually put a record on your turntable and listen straight through from beginning to end, then you may want to think twice about spending extra money for the programming capabilities we have described here. On the other hand, many CDs contain more selections than are found on LPs. There may be times when you will want to skip certain selections on a disc, and other times when you may just want to hear a few songs, instead of listening to the entire disc. If this is the case, you may indeed find that programmability is a worthwhile feature on a CD player.

FAST SEARCHING ON A COMPACT DISC

Many CD players allow you, at the touch of a button, to rapidly move from one point on a disc to another. Almost all players have a fast-search mode that permits you to skip ahead to the beginning of the next track, or backwards to the start of the track that's currently being played.

Some players go beyond that, and let you move ahead rapidly within a track, while you listen to a somewhat muted sampling of the material you are scanning. The sound you hear does not go up in pitch or produce the "chipmunk effect" that occurs when you fast forward an audiotape. Instead, you hear small portions of the sound, at the correct pitch and with a recognizable content, as the laser pickup assembly moves across the disc, hovering above its surface.

In less expensive machines, the fast-scanning process may be available in an inaudible version. You might be wondering how you can possibly know "where you are" during such fast scanning if you can't hear any sounds coming from the disc or CD player. Well, that brings us to the display area of CD players.

CD PLAYER DISPLAYS

Virtually every CD player has a display area, which is usually located to the right of the disc-loading drawer or elsewhere on the front panel of units that have a top-loading arrangement. Most units employ a liquid crystal display (LCD) or some form of fluorescent indicators. The LCD is generally found on portable CD players because it uses less power, imposing less of a drain on the batteries.

At the very least, the display indicates which track of a disc is currently being played. In addition, the display may tell you how much time has elapsed since the beginning of that track. More elaborate displays may also include the total number of available tracks and the total playing time of the disc; one or both of these are usually displayed when a disc is first mounted in the player and scanned by the laser pickup before play actually begins.

In the case of programmable CD players, there may be visual indications of the tracks that have been programmed into the player's memory, the program number being played, whether the repeat mode has been engaged, and other selected features. Many CD players will, at the push of a button, alternate between displaying the time that the current track has been playing and the total time remaining on the disc. If a player permits accessing by index points, index numbers will usually be displayed as well.

In the case of CD changers (yes, there are CD players that handle multiple discs; we'll examine some of them in Chapter 8), displays also show which of the discs loaded in the player is currently playing, as well as which discs and tracks are programmed for future play. Surprisingly, about the only thing we haven't seen in the display area of a CD player is a clock that tells you the correct time and date, but who knows, that may be coming next.

REMOTE CONTROL

Wireless remote-control units have become popular in home electronic products in recent years. Originally available for controlling channel selection and volume levels of television sets, there are now remote controls for VCRs, stereo receivers, and tape recorders, as well as units that control all (or most) of the components of integrated audio/video systems.

All of these remote-control modules operate using infrared light and encoded signals. These signals, picked up by an infrared light sensor located on the front panel of the component, are translated to the necessary electrical switching signal needed to initiate the desired function or action.

Even the very first CD player introduced in this country by Sony in 1983 featured a hand-held, wireless remote-control module. Today, most higher priced CD players include such remote-control units. Being able to control your CD player from the comfort of your chair or sofa, across the room from the player, is certainly convenient. Be aware, however, that not all remote controls supplied with CD players are the same; some can perform more functions than others.

The simplest type of remote control usually includes those controls needed to initiate, pause, and stop play, duplicating similar controls found on the front panel of the CD player itself. In addition, these basic remote-control modules are usually able to alter volume-control settings and perhaps even turn the CD player's power on and off. More elaborate remote-control units allow you to perform such functions as track-by-track advance or retard, fast search, and in some cases, audible fast search.

The most elaborate remote controls are those that are sometimes supplied with programmable CD players. These remote units, usually equipped with numeric keys, may allow you to program the player remotely, as if you were using the controls on the CD player's front panel. If you choose a player with a more elaborate remote-control module, you are likely to pay more for the CD player. Again, you should consider just how you intend to use the CD player. If your needs are limited to placing a disc inside the player, sitting down, and listening to the music from beginning to end, there is no reason to pay extra for a CD player that has a complex remote-control unit.

HEADPHONE OUTPUTS

Many of today's CD players are equipped with a front-panel headphone jack. Almost any pair of stereo headphones will work, but if you intend to listen to CDs through headphones, we would strongly recommend that you purchase a high-quality pair. After all, you wouldn't listen to your CDs using a pair of inferior loudspeakers, so you shouldn't impose a limitation on the sound quality you hear from your CD player by using cheap, inferior headphones.

Your audio dealer is probably best equipped to advise you on the headphones to use with your CD player. Audition headphones in much the same way that you would audition loudspeaker systems—by listening to a wide variety of music from demonstration CDs and comparing the fidelity of several sets of headphones under actual listening conditions.

In addition, consider the factor of comfort and style. Wearing headphones for several hours can be uncomfortable if they press too hard against your head, or if they are not easily adjusted to fit the contour of your head. Finally, choose between open-air headphones that allow outside sounds to reach your ears even when you are wearing the headphones, and circumaural headphones that completely surround your ears and block out any outside sounds.

If you elect to use headphones with your CD player, make certain that the player is equipped with a level control that affects the signal being sent to the headphone output jack. This control will allow you to adjust the volume of sound produced by the headphones without necessarily affecting the output level at the main (loudspeaker) output jacks. Some CD players also offer a control that varies the output level at the main output terminals. Such control may be useful if, as discussed in the previous chapter, the maximum voltage accepted by your amplifier's or receiver's high-level (AUX, TUNER, or TAPE) inputs is too low to handle the high levels of signal voltage delivered by most CD players.

Even if your amplifier or receiver is able to handle those high signal levels, you may still want the output control feature on your CD player. That way, you can adjust the output level of the CD player so that when you switch back and forth between, for example, your tuner, conventional records, tapes, and CDs, there won't be a big difference in the loudness levels. Without this adjustment, you might have to adjust the main volume control on your amplifier or receiver each time you switch back and forth between CDs and any other program source.

SUBCODE OUTPUTS: FOR FUTURE USE

The fact that CDs actually work is an amazing feat. After all, the digital system requires 705,600 bits (binary digits) of information per second, which are numerical representations of a tiny fraction, or sample, of the original analog sound. (That's the 16 bits necessary to represent a single amplitude sample of a musical waveform multiplied by 44,100, which is the number of samples taken each second.)

Since there are 3,600 seconds in an hour, and a CD can easily reproduce an hour of sound, that adds up to 2,540,160,000 bits of information (705,600 bits per second multiplied by 3,600 seconds) that are inscribed beneath the surface of a typical Compact Disc; simply stated, that's over 2½ billion bits! The floppy disks used with more advanced microcomputers, like the IBM Personal Computer AT, store about 5 million bits per side. Now you can understand the computer industry's interest in using CDs to store data.

CDs are truly amazing when you discover that each disc can store far more than the 2½ billion bits needed for sound. Some of the additional space is used for the information that controls the CD player and provides all of the excellent features that further differentiate CDs from phonograph records.

Using some mathematical wizardry, engineers created eight different *subcode channels,* which can be extracted from a CD and help your player act in an "intelligent" manner. These channels directly affect the operating features that are accessed by the front panel of the CD player, and were assigned letters of the alphabet from "P" through "W."

Channel "P" informs inexpensive CD players about the beginning and ending of selections, such as songs. Channel "Q" tells more sophisticated players all they need to know about a given CD, such as track numbers, index numbers, timings, frequency equalizations (known as *preemphasis*), and even if the disc contains four-channel sound. The "Q" channel also contains plenty of empty sections for future applications.

This explanation of the "P" and "Q" channels was not intended to make you a digital-audio engineer; it was discussed to give you some idea of the immense storage space contained in the standard for Compact Discs. Remember, we have only discussed what's being done (and what may be done) with the "P" and "Q" subcode channels. We haven't even touched on the possible uses for the "R," "S," "T," "U," "V," and "W" subcode channels, each of which has as much storage capacity as the "P" and "Q" channels.

In addition, the companies that developed this incredible recording format have not yet explored all of the possibilities. Every piece of literature we've obtained that discusses the CD format and its contents simply evades the subject by saying that subcode channels "R" through "W" have not been defined, and that the uses for them have not been determined. For the moment, they are being recorded as "binary 0," or total silence; that condition will soon change.

All sorts of uses, primarily visual, are being considered for this vast reserve of data storage capacity. Lyrics of songs could be projected on a TV screen as the music is reproduced from a Compact Disc. In future CD recordings, the complete librettos (text) of operas, in their original language, as well as in English or any other language, could be digitally encoded in the remaining subcode areas of the disc and displayed on a TV screen as you listen to the opera.

Demonstrations by several companies have already been held in which still pictures, derived from digital data encoded in CDs, were shown. Such still pictures can be "refreshed," or changed, about every thirteen seconds—that's how extensive the digital storage space is that remains unused on CDs today.

Is it too farfetched to predict that someday the unused space on Compact Discs could be used to tie together a video system, audio system, and a personal computer (the latter of which also "talks" in binary 0's and 1's)? Probably not. Perhaps this combination could deliver still pictures to fit the mood of the music, while at the same time controlling room lighting and other home appliances. It also seems quite reasonable to expect the small-sized CD to store moving video pictures, as well. In this age of electronic miracles, we are learning that most anything we dream up can become a reality; why should the amazing Compact Disc technology be any different?

INTERNAL DIFFERENCES BETWEEN CD PLAYERS

So much for the external features of CD players. Internally, there are also major design differences between players made by various firms and even between different models made by one company. To untrained listeners, most of these differences will not be very significant in terms of the quality of reproduced sound. Critical listeners, however, may be able to hear subtle differences between two CD players.

As you shop for a CD player, you are going to be bombarded with a series of "buzzwords." These include terms such as 16-bit versus 14-bit D/A (digital-to-analog) convertors, digital versus analog filtering, noise shaping, oversampling, quantization noise, and other unfamiliar words. Throughout this book, we will discuss only the more important terms.

Manufacturers that use different design techniques will also attempt to convince you that their particular approach is the best one, and the sound reproduced by their CD players is superior to that delivered by competitive products. Our purpose is not to take sides in the growing debate concerning the best way to design a CD player, but rather to explain the technical differences between the two basic approaches that seem to be emerging. You'll have to be the judge as to whether you can hear any differences between players built using one approach and those employing the alternate method.

WHY FILTERING IS NEEDED

You may recall that in the CD encoding process, analog signals are sampled at a rate of 44,100 times per second (44.1 kilohertz, or KHz). The theory of digital audio tells us that, in attempting to reconstruct the original signal during the decoding process, any frequencies higher than half the sampling frequency must not appear in the output. That means we must filter out everything above 20 KHz or so.

In a 16-bit system, such as that used for CDs, which has a sampling frequency of 44.1 KHz, the signal that the CD player derives from the disc must contain only the original audio frequencies and not the periodic repetitions of the audio frequencies that are produced by the sampling frequency (44.1 KHz) itself. The spectral distribution of these unwanted frequencies is illustrated in figure 3-1.

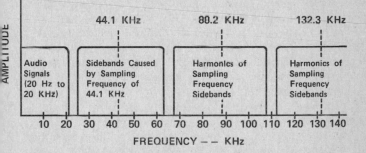

Figure 3-1. All frequencies above 20 KHz must be filtered out by the playback unit to prevent false decoding of the digital data.

Notice that the bottom end (farthest left) of these extra frequency bands is close to the audio frequency range, which ends at 20 KHz. Such extraneous, super-audible (above the range of human hearing) frequencies must be filtered out. Otherwise they might overload the amplifier, mix with the audio frequencies to produce unwanted "beats" (which produce various noises), or combine with tape recorder bias (inaudible, high-frequency signals that are required to properly record sounds on tape) to cause interference that you can hear.

If the sequence of pulses that represents the signal amplitudes as they are sampled is simply converted back to analog amplitudes, a series of spikes is produced, as shown in the top illustration of figure 3-2. While the outline of these spikes resembles the original audio wave, the constant on/off switching (the sampling at a rate of 44,100 times per second) produces the infinite series of undesirable frequency bands depicted in figure 3-1.

In practice, each sample is held in the digital-to-analog (D/A) convertor until the next sample arrives, producing a "step" waveform that more closely resembles the original audio waveform, as illustrated at the bottom of figure 3-2. Even so, significant components of the out-of-band (inaudible) frequencies still remain, particularly in the region near the top end of the audio band (near 20 KHz). While these frequencies can be detected by testing equipment, you normally cannot hear them.

Many CD player manufacturers suppress these unwanted frequency bands by using steep, sharp-cutoff analog filter circuits after the signal has been converted to analog form. Competing firms contend that such filtering degrades the signal's accuracy. While that may be subject to debate, there is no doubt that such filtering introduces *phase distortion*, or time delay, at the high-frequency end of the audio spectrum. In other words, treble (high-pitched) sounds reach your ears at a different time than bass (low-pitched) sounds. Many audio purists maintain that such phase distortion affects stereo imaging (the spatial sense that stereo projects) as well as the overall tonal quality of reproduced music.

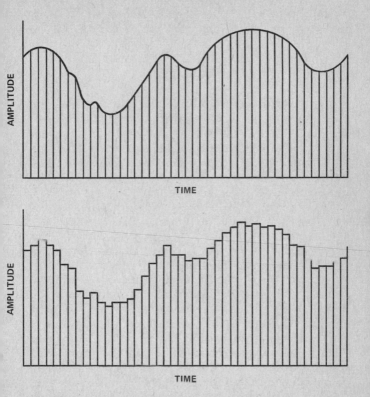

Figure 3-2. A series of pulses (top illustration), recovered during digital-to-analog decoding, produces step waveforms (bottom illustration) to approximate the original audio signal. The bottom waveform clearly shows that the amplitude of the signal does not change until the value for the next sample is encountered. When oversampling is used, the "steps" are closer together, resulting in a better replica (smoother curve) of the original waveform.

An alternative method used by many manufacturers uses digital, not analog, filters. Unlike the analog method, digital filtering occurs *before* the digital-to-analog (D/A) conversion process and does not introduce any phase distortion (time delay).

OVERSAMPLING

CD players that employ the digital filtering technique combine it with a digital-to-analog system called *oversampling*. This consists of multiplying the sampling frequency by a factor of two, or in some cases, by a factor of four. Therefore, 44.1 KHz (the normal sampling frequency for CDs) becomes 88.2 KHz or 176.4 KHz. The most immediate effect of oversampling is to suppress, or filter out, all of those lower frequency bands we saw in figure 3–1, namely those centered at 44.1 KHz, 88.2 KHz, and 132.3 KHz.

The final element in this digital filtering/oversampling scheme is a device known as a very gently sloping, analog, low-pass filter. This serves the purpose of removing the remaining nonaudible components in the band at frequencies of around 88.2 KHz or 176.4 KHz, and higher.

In the case of the analog, low-pass filter, the phase linearity of the reconstituted audio signal is more accurate, causing little or no time delay. For those who claim to hear the effects of phase error, this method should provide an advantage. Certainly, the two approaches (digital versus analog filtering) do result in different lab-measured results when certain signals are reproduced from a test disc.

On the other hand, some people maintain that under certain conditions (flat frequency response, low harmonic and modulation distortions, and high signal-to-noise ratios), phase errors are of little or no audible significance. We won't settle that argument here (it's been going on for decades), but you may want to make your own decision. This can be done by carefully auditioning CD players that employ each type of design, using identical Compact Discs, and rapidly switching from one player to the other.

ALTERNATIVE LASER BEAM PICKUPS

Another pair of design alternatives you are likely to encounter as you shop for a CD player has to do with the player's laser pickup and optical system. Some manufacturers claim that they are using a *"three-beam"* laser system and that this is inherently superior to the *"single-beam"* system. First, let's clarify what this means.

Every CD player we know of has only one laser within it. When manufacturers speak of a three-beam laser system, they simply mean that various lens and prism combinations are used to split the laser beam into three separate beams. The main, or central, beam is used to track (follow the path of) the digital-audio data beneath the surface of the CD. The two remaining beams, each displaced slightly to the left or right of the main beam, are used to guide the pickup assembly and keep it tracking accurately.

You see, in addition to the audio information, the microscopic pits beneath the surface of the disc also carry tracking, or guidance, signals for the laser pickup. Since the pickup assembly is not in physical contact with the surface of the disc and since there are no grooves to guide the pickup, a series of complex *servomechanisms* (controlling devices that automatically correct a unit's performance when it deviates from the norm) executes that function by "reading" the tracking data embedded in the disc.

In a single-beam system, one laser beam is focused to a point beneath the surface of the disc where the beam impinges on (strikes) both the digital-audio data *and* the tracking code data. Using a series of mirrors and other optical devices, mistracking (imperfect tracking) is detected by changes in the shape of the pattern of light reflected from beneath the surface of the disc. These changes in the light pattern cause variations in the signal levels sent to the servomechanisms that form a part of the laser pickup guidance system in single-beam CD players.

As you may have guessed, either a single-beam or three-beam system, if properly designed and built, can do an effective job of keeping the laser pickup assembly on track at all times. Nevertheless, there are differences in tracking accuracy and stability between different models and brands of CD players. However, these differences are not directly attributable to whether the CD player employs a three-beam or a single-beam pickup assembly.

DIGITAL-AUDIO MYTHS

Ever since *digitally mastered* LP records were released a few years ago, some audio "purists" have insisted that digital sound reproduction fails to convey musical accuracy to the same degree as analog sound reproduction. A few self-appointed experts have even suggested (in pseudo-scholarly papers) that listening to digitally mastered records can lead to stress, elevated heart rate, and high blood pressure!

Mind you, such physical symptoms were blamed not on CDs, which are truly digital; instead, they were attributed to "needle in the groove," analog LP records. The only difference between digitally mastered records and conventional ones is the fact that digitally mastered LPs are created from master tapes that were digitally recorded. The digitally mastered records themselves are as analog as any phonograph record made in the last hundred years!

If such myths could be created about digitally mastered records, it comes as no surprise that there would be even more myths and objections voiced concerning the radically new technology involved in making truly digital Compact Discs. In some quarters, the objections to CDs have been most violent.

Accusations have been made against the audio industry to the effect that the CD is a great "hoax," representing a 30-year regression in the history of good audio. We will not respond to such ludicrous generalizations. The fact that you are reading this book indicates that you have either heard the splendid musical accuracy reproduced from CDs or that you are interested in learning more about them. However, we would like to touch on a few specific points that have been raised about the new CD standards.

"WE NEED A HIGHER SAMPLING RATE"

If you've been following the development of digital audio, you've probably heard that plea more than once. As you may recall, the sampling rate is the number of times per second that an analog waveform is sampled, or looked at, for analog-to-digital conversion. In the earliest experiments in digital recording, conducted by companies such as Soundstream (under the able leadership of Dr. Tom Stockham), the sampling rate was 50 KHz. Now, the sampling rate used in most professional digital recordings (such as on reel-to-reel digital tape mastering equipment) is 48 KHz, while the sampling rate for CDs is "only" 44.1 KHz. Which sampling rate is "correct"?

It is a well-established theorem of information theory that in order to convert an analog waveform into its digital equivalent, the sampling rate must be at least twice that of the highest frequency you hope to reproduce. In the case of audio signals, if we want to reproduce audible frequencies as high as 20 KHz, the sampling rate must be at least 40 KHz. The 44.1 KHz sampling rate used for CDs was decided on in order to allow for some tolerance (deviation from a standard) in the components that make up the analog, low-pass filter that is needed to remove all unwanted signal components above 20 KHz.

Based on the above theorem and assuming that 20 KHz is the highest frequency humans can hear (no one has proven otherwise), the 44.1 KHz sampling rate chosen for the CD standard is high enough. The argument that a higher sampling rate would have been desirable to provide more latitude in the design of the low-pass filter may be valid, but arguing that a higher sampling rate would in and of itself lead to better reproduction of high frequencies is counter to the mathematically valid information theory.

"WE NEED A HIGHER BIT RATE"

It has been argued that a 16-bit digital "word" does not provide enough increments, or steps, for an accurate representation of sampled amplitudes in the analog-to-digital processing of an audio waveform. In fact, in Chapter 1 we showed that even a 14-bit code (as used in a digital-audio processor coupled to a home videocassette recorder for digital-audio taping) provided very little distortion and a high degree of dynamic range. Since the issue is constantly being raised with regard to CDs, let's see just what a 16-bit word provides by way of available numbers.

In something of an oversimplification, a 16-bit word means that the amount of numbers available to describe a waveform sample equals 2 raised to the 16th power (or 16 2's multiplied together); that multiplies out to 65,536 available numbers.

Now, suppose that in the analog-to-digital conversion, a waveform sample at a given instant was midway between level number 65,535 and 65,536. (The music was very loud indeed during that sample time.) The system would have to introduce a half-step error, choosing either the digital number 65,535 or 65,536, since there is no whole number available between those two. The error (distortion in the resulting waveform) would therefore be 0.5 divided by 65,536, or 0.00076%. Do you know of any amplifiers (or speakers, for that matter) that do as well? We don't.

To be perfectly fair, we should mention that the distortion in such digital systems is always lower at louder levels, as in the above example, since bit (binary digit) numbers for very loud volumes are at their highest level. If you reduce the volume by 40 dB, you have only $\frac{1}{100}$ th as many numbers with which to play. At 60 dB below the maximum recording level (referred to as -60 dB), there are only $\frac{1}{1000}$ th as many numbers with which to work; at that level, the maximum misrepresentation (error) of an amplitude would be "half a space," or 0.5 divided by 65.5, which equals 0.76% and is still a relatively low error.

There are other major and minor myths associated with this new technology. An important one—the claim of a 90 dB dynamic range—is clarified in Chapter 4, while other myths are simply not worth addressing seriously, such as the previously mentioned "listener stress and hypertension."

In evaluating the present state and future potential of the CD, it is wise to remember what the earliest stereophonic records sounded like in the late 1950s and early 1960s. Somehow, we were more willing to tolerate poor stereo recordings then, recognizing that the science of such recordings was bound to improve in time. Given the superb, noise-free, wide dynamic range of Compact Discs, it seems only fair that we now act at least as tolerant.

ERROR CORRECTION

Suppose you're playing a conventional LP record and the needle (stylus) of your phonograph pickup, for one reason or another, loses contact with the groove for a fraction of a second; this is not a big problem. All that you hear is a momentary muting, or absence of sound; then the music resumes, sometimes with a slight "pop" as the needle reestablishes contact with the record groove.

Similarly, when you play a tape recording, there will be a momentary "dropout" of information if there is a poor coating of the magnetic particles over a small area of tape; this also results in a brief absence of sound. In any analog-audio system, such brief interruptions of sound are hardly catastrophic.

Now, consider what happens when the laser pickup of a CD player fails to read one or more of the 0's or 1's in a sample code. Remember, each sample consists of 16 binary number combinations (0's and 1's).

Suppose that a certain sample should be read as "1111111111111111." In binary numbering, that corresponds to the maximum signal level possible (the loudest sound sample that can be recorded on a CD); in decimal numbering, that equals 65,535. If the laser pickup misreads the first of those 1's, the pickup would interpret the sample as having a value "0111111111111111;" that is only half the amplitude (32,767) of the true value of the sample (65,535). This very gross error, if uncorrected, would produce a crashing, spike-like sound in your loudspeaker. What's more, if several such errors occurred in a short time, the resulting sound reproduction would be highly distorted and unlistenable.

Fortunately, the designers of the CD system foresaw such problems, and they developed an error-correction system that is very complex and beyond the scope of this book. Suffice it to say that through a system of checks and double checks, plus redundant (multiple) encoding and interleaving of samples, a typical CD can have as many as 4,000 data dropouts in a row, and when you play it, you won't hear anything wrong. (That many dropouts are not unlikely, as in the case of a scratched disc or one that is very dirty and has opaque areas on its surface through which the laser beam cannot penetrate.)

The error-correction schemes used in CDs are divided into several levels. Therefore, a CD player may utilize some or all of the error-correction potential built into the system, depending on how much the manufacturer wants to spend on error-detection and error-correction circuitry. As you might expect, CD players in different price categories exhibit varying degrees of error-correction capability.

Checking out this characteristic of a CD player is not easy, since it is difficult for you to find a CD having a known number and frequency of dropouts. In our tests of CD players, we use a special disc with calibrated dropouts that simulate scratches on the surface of a disc, dirt or dust particles, and even fingerprint smudges. We'll have more to say about these and other tests in the next chapter.

However, it is easy for you to judge the CD player's tracking stability, as well as its resistance to external vibration and shock. This is done by lightly tapping the housing, or cabinet, of the CD player on its top and sides with your finger.

All CD Players Are Not Equal

Better CD players—or at least those with superior tracking stability—will play right through such testing without missing a beat. Inferior mechanisms may mistrack when external tapping is done; you will hear either a moment of interrupted sound, or the laser pickup assembly will skip and move to another portion of the recorded program.

With a bit of practice, you will be able to tap each CD player with the same amount of force (don't use too much). That way, you'll be able to separate the more stable, shock-resistant units from those that mistrack when subjected to the least amount of external vibration or shock. Be sure to obtain the dealer's permission before you tap on the equipment; if there is any objection, ask if he or she could do the tapping for you, although it's best, for the sake of consistency, if you perform the test.

TAKING CARE OF YOUR CD PLAYER AND DISCS

CD players require little or no maintenance. If the CD player that you purchase comes with one or more "locking screws" that must be removed before you start to use the player, be sure to retain those screws in a safe place. If ever you need to transport the CD player, or ship it to a service facility, it is very important that you reinstall and tighten the locking screws. This firmly secures the delicate laser pickup assembly so that it won't be damaged, or even ripped loose, during transportation of the unit.

Aside from this simple procedure, there is almost nothing that you need to do to keep your CD player in perfect working condition. Of course, you will want to dust off its cabinet, or outer case, from time to time, but don't remove the outer case to clean inside the unit. For one thing, removal of the cabinet may void any warranties offered by the manufacturer.

Secondly, once the CD player is opened, you may be tempted to defeat the mechanism that makes it impossible for the laser beam to be turned on when the disc drawer is open. While the laser beam used in CD players produces only microwatts of (very weak) laser energy, direct exposure to this coherent, intense light beam could damage your eyesight or otherwise pose a health hazard. It's nothing to worry about so long as the machine is fully assembled; manufacturers must have their products rigidly tested for safety by government agencies before they are approved for sale. Such tests do not guarantee safety, however, if you open up the unit and tamper with its insides.

If your CD player ever requires servicing, do not try to repair it yourself. Bring (or ship) it to a service station that is approved by the manufacturer of your CD player. The store where you bought the machine may offer their own service (make sure it is factory-authorized), or they should be able to refer you to such an organization. Remember to reinstall and tighten the locking screws; to further protect the unit, always put it in the original carton and packing material (some manufacturers will void the warranty if these two steps are not taken).

COMPACT DISCS ARE NOT INDESTRUCTIBLE

Those amazing CDs, which have been touted as being able to last forever, are not nearly as indestructible as some of the promoters of CDs would have you believe. Yes, we've seen the demonstrations of the discs being dropped on a dirty floor and then played flawlessly, with that incredible laser pickup system focusing and reading right through the dust.

But take our advice: Handle the discs much as you would an LP, holding them only by their edges. Keep them free of dust (use a lint-free cloth), and don't let them get scratched by allowing them to lie around outside of their plastic containers. No amount of hand polishing or cleaning will get rid of a deep scratch in a CD. And such scratches can cause sporadic audio muting (absence of sound), repetition of a musical phrase (reminiscent of a "broken record" sound), or even total failure of the laser pickup to find the desired selection and begin playing.

Minor surface scratches on a CD may go totally unnoticed during playback due to the sophisticated error-correction schemes built into the CD system. However, if the scratches are severe, the error-correction circuitry may not be able to "smooth over" the data that the laser pickup can no longer read.

Interestingly, not all CD players are able to correct errors or supply missing data to the same degree. That's because the CD standards offer a wide degree of latitude as to just how the error-correction schemes are to be incorporated. A manufacturer that wants to economize or produce a lower cost player may incorporate only one of the available levels of error correction, while another maker may incorporate every available error-correction scheme, even if that means coming up with a more expensive player.

Occasionally, you may run into a CD that is defective in some way. Your first inclination will probably be to blame the CD player when mistracking occurs, but before you jump to any conclusions, try another disc in the same machine. If the second disc plays perfectly, the trouble may well be with the first disc itself, and not the player. In this respect, CDs are no different from LP records.

Once in a while you're going to run into a bad "pressing." When you consider the microscopic dimensions involved in the injection-molding process that impresses the "pits" into CDs, it's amazing that the field rejection rate reported recently by Polygram (one of the two major CD production facilities in the world) is as low as it is; an incredible 0.3% of all discs shipped. Still, you may be unfortunate enough to get one of the very rare defective discs.

One marvelous side benefit arises from the method used to play CDs. Since there is absolutely no wear on a CD when it is played, dealers are often willing to let you audition a disc that you intend to buy before you pay for it. That being the case, if you and the dealer have the time, you can play the entire disc and leave the store completely certain that the CD you have purchased is not defective.

Over the short span of time since CDs were first introduced, we've learned a lot about their strong points—and their weak points. For example, we now know that the label side is actually more prone to damage than the clear side through which the laser pickup actually reads those billions of pits that constitute the digital-audio signal. The reason for this is that the protective layer on the disc's label side is much thinner than it is on the clear side.

We've also learned that CDs, far from being indestructible, are very easily scratched, and that when such scratches exceed a certain width or depth, all the error-correction circuitry in the world will not prevent the laser pickup from skipping all over the disc, or at the very least, repeating a musical phrase over and over again, unable to find the guidance information needed to keep it on track.

Since CDs impart their information to a laser pickup, the ability of that pickup to transmit and receive reflected light to and from a plane (flat) surface beneath the clear, protective plastic coating of the disc is essential. Transparency of the plastic surface can be impaired not only by scratches, but by dirt, smudges, fingerprint oils, and any other foreign substance that renders the surface of the disc partially or completely opaque.

CLEANING THE DISCS

Ask the developers of Compact Discs what sort of disc cleaning or maintenance they recommend, and both Philips and Sony will tell you all that's needed is a lint-free, dry, chamois-like cloth, which should be used occasionally to wipe off fingerprints and dust particles that may be adhering to the surface of the disc. It is very important to note that the "chamois" or "chamois-like cloth" is *not* the animal hide that many people use to dry off their windows and cars. This rough animal skin could scratch and permanently damage your CDs. The "chamois" that is included in many CD cleaning kits and with some CD players is a soft, felt-like, synthetic material that is specially designed for cleaning CDs. Both companies will also stress that the wiping should be done radially, that is, in straight lines from the center of the disc, moving outward. This is just the way consumers have been warned *not* to clean their conventional, grooved LPs.

If you think about it, the radial, linear cleaning strokes make more sense for a CD. Even the finest lint-free cloth may leave some minute scratches on the polished, transparent plastic surface of a CD. If those scratches are oriented from the inside of the disc outward, they cross the digital information tracks and the amount of opacity is minuscule, so that most error-correction schemes can safely overcome it. However, if tiny scratches follow the circular tracks of the digital information, even the narrowest opaque scratch might obliterate thousands upon thousands of digital "samples," resulting in mistracking.

Despite the recommendations of both developers of the CD format, many manufacturers of accessory items have seen fit to develop and market CD cleaning kits. Most, but not all, of these products include a cleaning solution, which is applied to the disc either manually or by some form of spraying device. It should be noted that at least two manufacturers of CD software (recorded discs) told us that if a solution must be used for cleaning CDs, probably the safest and most effective liquid to use would be alcohol.

The only problem we could foresee is the possibility that the liquid will not be effectively removed from the surface of the disc. If the CD is played before it is completely dry, there may be problems, including possible damage to the player. This danger applies, to a lesser or greater extent, to all cleaning kits that use any sort of liquid. Many of the brochures supplied with the kits warn of this possibility, and stress the fact that discs must be completely dry before you play them.

We have investigated some of the more popular CD cleaners now being promoted by various manufacturers. When properly used, the CD cleaning kits that we evaluated did not cause any serious damage to the CDs. Discs that were wet after cleaning dried with visible stains that resembled water spots, but in no case did such stains cause any mistracking.

CHAPTER 4

How We Tested the CD Players

As you read the test reports in the next few chapters, you may wonder how we were able to quantify the test results to such a fine degree. After all, there weren't too many audio components that had harmonic distortion levels of a mere 0.003% or less until the advent of the Compact Disc. (Total harmonic distortion, or THD, is the amount of extraneous material that is a multiple of the desired frequency. For example, a 2 KHz audio signal may produce unwanted frequencies at 4 KHz, 6 KHz, and 8 KHz. These harmonics, or overtones, are byproducts of digital audio, and they create distortion that you can hear, so they must be filtered out.)

A conventional phonograph cartridge having a frequency response that deviated by no more than (plus or minus) 3.0 dB over the entire audio frequency range (20 Hz to 20 KHz) was considered to be quite good. (Frequency response reflects a device's ability to handle the frequencies that are applied to it.) Contrast this with CD players exhibiting response characteristics that are flat (uniform) to within a small fraction of one decibel from 20 Hz to 20 KHz. Stereo separation reproduced by even the best phonograph cartridges seldom exceeded 30 dB or so, whereas in the case of CD players, stereo separation between channels can be 80 or even 90 decibels!

In the early stages of CD production, there were very few test discs with which to evaluate Compact Disc players. Soon afterward, both codevelopers of the CD system began to issue specially prepared test discs, which contained a variety of signals that could be used to test the performance of a CD player.

Sony makes at least two test discs, while Philips offers a set of three discs for laboratory test purposes. The first of these Philips discs has 27 separate tracks of test signals; we'll describe most of them shortly. The remaining two discs are known as "Test Sample 4" and "Test Sample 4A." Both contain identical musical selections, but Test Sample 4A also has an opaque wedge (to imitate a scratch), three black dots of increasing diameter (to simulate dust specks), and a semitransparent "smudge" to simulate a fingerprint. This disc is used to check a CD player's error-correction and tracking capabilities, since these features vary from one design to another.

Since the test signals on the Sony and Philips discs are digitally created and recorded (rather than being translated from analog signals to a digital form), there is no doubt as to whether less-than-perfect readings are due to the disc or to the player being tested. In this respect, these test discs are far superior to the test records used to evaluate turntables or phonograph cartridges.

THE TESTS THEMSELVES

Although we now have several other sources of test signals for checking frequency response, we prefer to use the Philips disc's sweep signals. These continuously variable signals start at very low frequencies (about 20 Hz) and gradually go up (sweep) to high frequencies (20,000 Hz or so).

A laboratory test instrument (Sound Technology 1500A) can "track" this sweep accurately, and display the sweep in graphic form on its video screen; we can also get a printout of the response. Furthermore, this test instrument lets us expand the vertical scale so that one vertical division equals 2 decibels, instead of the usual 10 dB. If this were not done, the frequency responses of all CD players, which are nearly perfect, would appear as straight lines.

The Philips disc also has nine "spot" frequencies (specific frequencies, as opposed to continuously variable sweep signals) for measuring the harmonic distortion at 0 dB (the maximum recording level). These frequencies are repeated at -24 dB and -30 dB (i.e., 24 dB and 30 dB below the maximum recording level). All other things being equal, distortion at the -24 dB level should be 24 dB worse (about ten times as bad) than it is at the 0 dB level, and should double again when going from -24 dB to -30 dB (a 6 dB change represents a doubling of distortion).

A series of 997 Hz tones follows the nine spot frequencies on the Philips disc, coming at progressively decreasing amplitudes, from 0 dB all the way down to -90 dB. These are used to check the overall linearity of a CD player. This means that you test to see if a change in the input signal (i.e., the signal being "read" by the CD player from the disc) is reflected by the same amount of change in the output signal (i.e., the signal coming out of the CD player and being fed into your amplifier). For instance, if there is a 1.0-volt change in the input signal, there should also be a 1.0-volt change in the output signal. Linearity is often a problem when the music goes from a very loud volume level to a very soft one.

In general, all the CD players we tested were quite linear at least down to around -80 dB. Below that level, it was difficult to determine whether any discrepancies in levels were the result of actual nonlinearities or simply due to the residual noise in the player and/or the measuring instrumentation. Frequency response sweeps, as well as tones for measuring both THD (total harmonic distortion) and linearity are all repeated on the Philips disc for the alternate (left and right) stereo channels.

The Sony and Philips test discs contain twin-tone signals for measuring intermodulation (IM) distortion. IM distortion results when two or more frequencies, which are being reproduced simultaneously, react with each other to produce additional sum or difference frequencies. For example, if a musical selection has tones at frequencies of 9,000 and 10,000 Hz, spurious (false, or misleading) components may appear at 1,000 Hz (the difference between the two frequencies) and at 19,000 Hz (the sum of the two frequencies).

Channel separation is best measured using the Sony test disc. This involves four test frequencies (100 Hz, 1 KHz, 10 KHz, and 20 KHz), which are first provided at the left-channel output while the right channel is set at "infinity zero" (totally silent, because all of the bits, or binary digits, are 0's). Then the four test frequencies are fed to the right channel, with the left-channel output set at infinity zero. A typical plot, or graph, of separation versus frequency can be derived from these tests.

SIGNAL-TO-NOISE RATIO TESTS

One of the most important advantages of the CD is its ability to reproduce music without any background noise or hiss. This is the attribute most people notice the first time they listen to a CD. Most of us have come to expect that ever-present, low-level surface noise (in the case of a phonograph record) or hiss (from a tape). When you listen to a CD, suddenly that noise is gone— you hear only the music.

However, if you turn up the volume on your amplifier (or receiver) to its highest setting, during the quietest portions of a musical selection you might be able to detect the slightest bit of background noise from some CD players. On the other hand, other machines will not produce any audible noise, no matter how high you set your volume control.

To measure the signal-to-noise (S/N) ratio of a CD player, the level of residual noise generated by the player is compared to the highest signal level (loudest music) that the CD player will ever produce. In digital terms, the loudest level that can be created from any CD is the level corresponding to a peak digital signal code consisting of sixteen 1's. (You will recall that this is the highest sample number that a 16-bit digital encoding system can read; it corresponds to a decimal value of 65,535.)

The total absence of sound, on the other hand, corresponds to a sample consisting of sixteen 0's. To measure signal-to-noise ratio, therefore, we play a test disc track in which only 0's have been encoded. If everything worked perfectly on all CD players, they would all exhibit the same S/N ratio.

However, since noise can be generated in other ways inside a CD player, there will be differences in the signal-to-noise ratios of various CD players. Typically, most of the CD players we tested exhibit S/N ratios well above 90 dB, with some approaching the incredibly good signal-to-noise ratio of 100 dB!

TRANSIENT RESPONSE AND PHASE RESPONSE TESTS

These tests involve oscilloscope observations, rather than meter readings and graphic plots. The Philips test disc offers other signals (square wave, impulse, and phase-checking), besides the already discussed sinusoidal (sine wave) signals, such as those used to check frequency response;   all of these signals are digitally created.

A typical example of how a square wave appears at the output of a CD player that uses so-called steep, analog output filtering is shown in figure 4-1. The square wave's appearance tells us something about the type of filtering being used in a specific CD player.

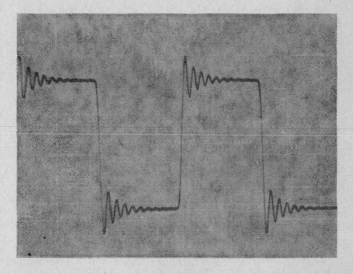

Figure 4-1. Oscilloscope photo showing typical 1 KHz square wave reproduction from a CD player that employs steep, analog output filters.

As discussed in Chapter 3 ("Why Filtering Is Needed"), most early CD players and quite a few of the newer, low-priced models use steep, analog output filter circuits to remove unwanted frequencies above 20,000 Hz. Such steep filtering is always accompanied by phase error, or time delay. This means that high-frequency components of the music are delayed by a finite number of microseconds, with respect to the middle- and low-frequency components. That is, the high-pitched, treble tones arrive at your ears later than the low-pitched, bass tones. Many experts and trained listeners maintain that this phase delay detracts from musical realism. Among other things, they claim it destroys some of the stereo imaging, or spatial perspective, of the reproduced music.

Newer CD players, especially those costing a bit more, utilize digital filtering prior to digital-to-analog conversion. As previously discussed, digital filtering is coupled with the oversampling technique. This means that instead of "reading" samples at the rate of 44,100 times per second (44.1 KHz, which is encoded on the disc itself), the CD player's circuitry operates at double that rate (88.2 KHz), or in some cases, four times as fast (176.4 KHz).

The simplest way to understand oversampling is to think of it as though the CD player's circuitry is reading each sample from the disc either two or four times. The net effect of oversampling is to eliminate the need for steep output filters; gentler filters, which introduce less phase error, can be used.

Impulse (or pulse) signals on the Philips disc simulate a very fast pulse (transient variation in the signal), as occurs in, for example, a quick drum beat. These signals use one sample ($\frac{1}{44100}$ of a second) that is at full scale (i.e., the highest intensity, or amplitude) or at $\frac{1}{10}$ full scale, while the next 127 samples are at "0" amplitude. The result appears in figure 4–2 for the same player whose square wave output was shown in figure 4–1. (While these two outputs aren't necessarily related, in general, if a CD player produces a good square wave, it is likely to also generate a good pulse.)

Various phase-response test signals are also included on the Philips disc. In our tests, we have never found a CD player in which the left- and right-channel

Figure 4–2. Oscilloscope photo showing a single pulse, as reproduced by the same CD player that generated the square wave in figure 4-1.

output signals were inadvertently wired "out of phase." If signals are out of phase, one signal might be negative while the other is positive, when they both should be, for instance, negative. As a result, the right loudspeaker's cone might be moving in while the left speaker's cone is going out; this can result in diminished bass tones. Using a test signal that has 2,000 Hz on one channel and 20,000 Hz on the other, it is quite easy to distinguish varying amounts of phase delays at high frequencies, depending on the CD player being tested.

How We Tested the CD Players

A STANDARD TEST DISC

Recently, the Electronic Industries Association of Japan (EIAJ) developed some standards for measuring the performance of CD players. A standardized test disc, which would contain all of the required test signals, was to be released along with the published standards; that disc has now been issued. Since the disc combines many of the signals that were formerly available only from several test discs, the task of the player tester has been somewhat simplified. Still, even the EIAJ test disc and its associated standards do not cover every possible test that might be required to thoroughly evaluate a CD player.

A standards subcommittee, operating under the sponsorship of the Electronic Industries Association (EIA), which is based in the U.S., is currently completing its work. They will soon be issuing their own standards for measuring and testing CD players. Most of the EIA standards will adopt the testing methods called for by the EIAJ, but a few extra tests may be added to differentiate more thoroughly between the performance of different CD players.

ERROR-CORRECTION TESTS

Remaining "bench tests" conducted for each CD player that passes through our laboratory deal with error correction, as well as tracking accuracy and stability. These tests utilize the Philips Test Sample 4A disc, which was described earlier.

The opaque wedge inscribed on the surface of this disc varies in width from 400 to 900 microns. (One micron, or micrometer, equals one millionth of a meter, or roughly 0.00004 inch.) This wedge is meant to simulate an opaque scratch that might be on a disc that had not been cared for properly. The black dots on the Test Sample 4A disc are used to simulate dust particles, ranging in width from 300 to 800 microns.

These widths can be related to specific musical tracks, so that by listening for any mistracking or audio muting (absence of sound), and noting the point on a given track that the disturbance occurred, it is easy to ascertain just how "wide" a defect the CD player's internal systems were able to handle without impairing the musical content. It is during these tests that we have observed the greatest differences between various makes and models of CD players.

THE MOST IMPORTANT TESTS OF ALL

After all the lab measurements and observations have been made, we conduct the most important tests of all. These are the listening tests, conducted in a reasonably quiet room that is properly furnished and acoustically treated for listening to music. It is the same room in which we have been testing and listening to audio equipment for nearly 15 years, and is therefore very familiar to our staff, including our engineers. Often, but not always, other critical listeners are called in to join us in the final evaluations of the equipment.

Now the problem becomes the choice of software, that is, the recorded discs. The supply of well-engineered discs that also contain tastefully recorded music is growing daily, and we now feel that we have a sufficient number of good CD recordings with which to judge the Compact Disc players.

To date, we have been unable to come up with "clear winners" in the CD player evaluations. All of the machines that we tested deliver superior sound quality. If we could listen to all of the CD players, side by side, using our latest selection of discs, we might be able to detect some subtle differences between players; unfortunately, that is not possible. Even so, we would need duplicates of each disc we wanted to use, since the differences between machines would probably be too subtle for us to judge, unless we could play two identical CDs in two players at once and switch from one to the other quickly.

Because all the machines deliver superior sound, the first sections in each of the test reports—the paragraphs that describe the operating and convenience features of each CD player—are just as important as the final sections that report the results of our lab and listening tests. This reflects our findings that, at this time, the major differences between CD players are in their operating features and physical layouts rather than in their sound quality.

CHAPTER 5

Home CD Player Reviews

Playing phonograph records demands involvement on your part, in that you have to get up and walk across the room to turn over the LP or skip songs that are not to your liking. Virtually all of the options offered with a conventional turntable are for performance. The only convenience feature is having the arm lift up at the end of an album's side and, normally, having the turntable shut off automatically. Performance choices are many, ranging from speed adjustments to alterations of the tonearm's vertical-tracking angles.

Home CD players, on the other hand, have many conveniences, while offering relatively few sound and performance adjustments. You don't have to turn over the single-sided CD, and by touching a few buttons, you decide which tracks (and their order) you will hear. An alphanumeric display shows various statistics about the CD that's in the player, while wireless remote control lets you take command from across the room. The few performance choices include how rapidly and accurately the player works, and whether it uses analog or digital filters to remove unwanted, audible byproducts of digital audio.

Most home turntables require a position of honor in the stereo system, because they usually load from the top and include a clumsy dust cover. Home CD players, however, are generally the same size and shape as your other components (e.g., receiver and tape deck). Since most CD players use a front-drawer loading mechanism, you can place the player anywhere in your stack of components. Compared to a turntable, this saves a lot of space. Also, CD players tend not to be as fussy about being perfectly level (horizontal) as do turntables.

Banish the impression that CD players are commodity items to be purchased on the basis of price alone. Every manufacturer puts its own distinctive imprint on its line of CD players.

For instance, the Pioneer PD-9010X packs numerous conveniences into a superb-sounding unit that sells for a relatively low price, while Denon offers superior stereo separation and sound in its machine. Sony's CD players boast top-notch performance, with some units offering "shuffle play," which plays the tracks on the disc in an ever-changing order. You can adjust stereo separation and dynamic range to your liking with dbx's CD player, while the Carver CD Player lets you alter the tonal balance and stereo perspective of early, less-than-perfect CD recordings.

Other examples of unique features can be seen in units made by Bang & Olufsen, which tend to mix sublime styling with ease of operation, whereas Revox outfits its rugged CD player with sophisticated programming functions. Shure offers a competitively priced CD player that strikes a proper balance between the action of digital filters and that of analog filters, while the Akai player accepts programming commands that closely resemble plain English. Technics loads its budget-priced player with most of the features seen in more expensive, competitive units, and Toshiba tempts you with a model that doubles as a home or portable player. Magnavox, on the other hand, offers the quality you expect from its parent company, Philips, at a very low price.

Therefore, whatever your needs or desires, it's likely there's a home CD player for you in this chapter. If you are looking for a portable, car, or multiple-disc CD player, check out the reviews in the following chapters. Note that all of the reviews are arranged in decreasing order of value, with the "Best Buys" listed first. However, be assured that no matter which CD player you choose, it will be one that we consider to be a good value.

PIONEER PD-9010X

Pioneer Electronics (USA) Inc.

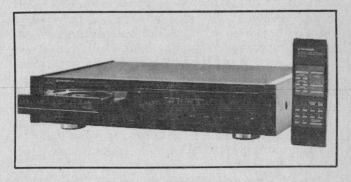

MANUFACTURER'S SPECIFICATIONS:

Frequency Response: 2 Hz to 20 KHz, ±0.5 dB.
Signal-to-Noise Ratio: 96 dB.
Dynamic Range: 96 dB.
Total Harmonic Distortion: 0.003% (1 KHz, 0 dB).
Channel Separation: 95 dB at 1 KHz.
Number of Programmable Events: 32 of a possible 99 tracks.
Audio Output Level: Fixed, 2.0 volts.
Dimensions: 17 $^{15}/_{16}$ Wide x 3¾ High x 12 $^{13}/_{16}$ inches Deep.
Approximate Retail Price: $540.
Approximate Low Price: $494.

Home CD Player Reviews

The list of superb "third-generation" CD players continues to grow. Pioneer's top unit for the current season is not only reasonably priced (relatively speaking, for a top-of-the-line CD player), but it is also their most feature-laden player to date.

You can program the PD-9010X to play up to 32 randomly accessed tracks on a disc, with the track numbers extending up to 99! A wireless, 13-function remote control is included, as is a front-panel stereo headphone jack that has a volume-level control.

In order to keep the front panel free of the profusion of buttons and knobs found on some competing players, Pioneer transfers the programming numeric keys to the remote control. In other words, you cannot use the front panel to program the unit for random accessing of the disc's tracks. You can, however, play discs in the normal fashion, using the front-panel buttons and controls.

Fast search and fast advance (or reverse) of the laser pickup from track to track is possible, and you can access a given point on a disc by its index number, if the CD is coded with such index points.

The display area provides you with a great deal of information. There are indicators for "Repeat Play," "Track" and "Index," "Minutes" and "Seconds" (of either time remaining or elapsed time), "Play," "Pause," "Disc" (to show that a CD has been properly loaded into the disc tray), and a "Remote Control" command acknowledgment. In addition to the large numerals that display the current track being played, 15 small numerals, arranged in a row below the main display, show the total number of tracks on the disc. An arrow pointing to the right indicates that the CD has more than 15 tracks.

CONTROL PANEL LAYOUT

The "Power" on/off switch and the stereo headphone jack with its level control are located along the left edge of the front panel. The slide-out disc tray is further to the right. While the disc tray can be opened and closed using the "Open/Close" pushbutton just to its right, the tray can also be closed by gently pushing its front surface after a disc is in place. Two small indicator lights to the side of the drawer show when a disc has been loaded and when a remote-control command has been received via the remote-sensor area on the front panel.

The elaborate display area is immediately to the right of the disc tray's "Open/Close" switch, while further to the right, near the panel's right-hand edge, are "Play" and "Pause" buttons. Controls along the lower part of the front panel include a "Time" key (which toggles the display between elapsed time, remaining time, and total time on a disc), a "Repeat" key, two "Index" search keys, a pair of manual search keys for fast-forward and fast-reverse searching, two track advance and reverse keys, and a "Stop/Clear" key that is used to discontinue play or clear the CD player's memory of any programmed instructions.

The hand-held remote-control unit supplied with the Pioneer PD-9010X duplicates most of the function keys described. It also has the "0" through "9" numeric keys mentioned earlier, plus a "Program" key for random-access programming of the CD player.

OUR LAB MEASUREMENTS

Frequency response of the Pioneer PD-9010X was very nearly flat to 20 KHz, measuring less than half a decibel down at that frequency extreme, which is a very good response. The harmonic distortion produced by this well-designed CD player was truly negligible. Harmonic distortion at 1 KHz was incredibly low, well below Pioneer's claims for noise plus total harmonic distortion (THD). The figures for intermodulation (IM) distortion were equally impressive.

The signal-to-noise ratio was considerably better than that claimed by Pioneer, but stereo separation was somewhat less than stated by the manufacturer. Aside from its many other sonic virtues, the PD-9010X is virtually free of any phase, or time-delay, errors normally attributed to analog output filters.

ERROR CORRECTION AND TRACKING

As we expected, the Philips "defects" disc was unable to trip up the excellent tracking and error-correction capabilities of this Pioneer CD player. As has been true of nearly all of the "third-generation" CD players we've tested, this unit had no trouble playing right through the simulated scratches (up to 900 microns in width), the simulated dust specks (up to 800 microns in diameter), and the simulated fingerprint smudge that extends over two complete musical tracks of the test disc.

The unit's resistance to mild vibration and external shock was especially good. The PD-9010X continued to play with no audible interruptions, skipping, or disc rejection while we subjected it to tapping along its top and side surfaces. Pioneer's engineers tell us that part of this stability comes from this CD player's unique internal-suspension system.

Another example of the care and attention given to this design is the special disc-retaining surface that engages CDs when they are being played. Most of disc-retaining surfaces in other CD players simply grab the disc near its center hole. In the Pioneer PD-9010X, nearly three quarters of the surface of a disc is supported while being played. This reduces error-causing vibration and disc warpage.

SUMMARY

The Pioneer PD-9010X is one of the most value-laden CD players we have evaluated to date. Every programming and display feature that might be useful to a listener has been included. All of those convenience features wouldn't be worth much, however, if the player lacked good sound reproduction capability. Not only is this player a superb-sounding instrument, but Pioneer has somehow managed to put all of these desirable qualities together in a machine that sells for a relatively affordable price.

SONY CDP-302II

Sony Corp. of America

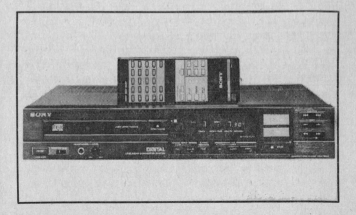

MANUFACTURER'S SPECIFICATIONS:

Frequency Response: 2 Hz to 20 KHz, ±0.5 dB.
Signal-to-Noise Ratio: 96 dB.
Dynamic Range: 96 dB.
Total Harmonic Distortion: Less than 0.003%.
Channel Separation: 95 dB.
Number of Programmable Events: 16.
Audio Output Level: Fixed, 2.0 volts rms.
Dimensions: 17 Wide x 3¼ High x 13¼ inches Deep.
Approximate Retail Price: $550.
Approximate Low Price: $494.

In their first two generations of CD players, Sony insisted on using steep, analog multipole filters at the output of their digital-to-analog convertors. They maintained that this approach was better able to suppress residual noise at the player's output, even if it did introduce rather severe phase shift at the upper end of the audible spectrum (around 20 KHz). Indeed, the argument as to whether high-frequency phase shift is of audible significance has never really been resolved. Some listeners are convinced that they can hear this form of "distortion," while others insist it is inaudible.

With the introduction of Sony's CDP-302II and other third-generation CD players, the argument becomes somewhat academic. Sony seems to have solved the problem with a "best of both worlds" solution. The CDP-302II incorporates what Sony calls their "Ultralinear D/A Converter"—a chip that includes a true 16-bit digital-to-analog convertor with double oversampling, as well as new digital filters that reject noise. The result is not only negligible phase shift, but also superior output linearity (even at very low signal levels), as well as incredibly flat frequency response from one end of the audible spectrum to the other.

Note that the CDP-302II is an upgraded version of Sony's CDP-302. The newer CDP-302II adds a timer switch and it uses a new ceramic material in the construction of the player's linear motor. Otherwise, the CDP-302II is the same as the CDP-302.

The relatively inexpensive CDP-302II is loaded with features that just a year ago would have been found on units costing at least twice as much. Aside from the fact that a full-function, hand-held wireless remote control is supplied, the CDP-302II is able to seek music by track or index number. Random access by track and index number is also possible, as is sequential programming by track or index number (in any random order) for up to 16 selections. Programs can be repeated, as can an entire disc, a given track, or any preselected continuous musical segment.

As with earlier Sony CD players, the rear panel has a subcode output for future use with an adaptor, allowing you to view CD graphics on your video system. For all its front-panel and rear-panel features, the Sony CDP-302II is a relatively compact unit. It weighs approximately 15 pounds and consumes only 15 watts of electricity, not counting any power drawn from its rear-panel auxiliary AC receptacle.

CONTROL PANEL LAYOUT

The front-loading drawer of the CDP-302II is flanked by a power switch, headphone jack with volume-level control on the left, and an open/close button on the right. The display area to the right of the drawer shows the track number being played, along with the elapsed playing time of that track or the total remaining play time for the entire disc, depending on the setting of an "Elapsed/Remaining" touch-switch, which is located below the display. If a given disc is divided into index numbers as well as tracks, both will be displayed as they are played.

The word "Disc" is shown when a CD is rotating in the drawer, while the word "Scan" is illuminated when the player's laser pickup searches for the point on the disc that you have programmed. Sony might just as well have omitted that last indication, since their new linear pickup motor and low-mass miniaturized laser pickup assembly locate a desired point on a disc so rapidly that you barely have time to look up from the front panel (or the keypad on your remote control) before the music begins to play.

Incidentally, while random-access programming cannot be done from the remote control, that hand-held unit does permit you to quickly get to any track by pressing only one or two buttons on its 23-key pad. The new small laser pickup assembly used in the CDP-302II was designed originally for Sony's portable D-5 (since replaced by their D-7) and their new car CD players, where it does an equally effective job of locating desired points on a CD in less than 1 second.

Below the display area are the repeat programming buttons and the touch buttons required for random programming of selections. "Pause" and "Play" buttons are located to the right of the display area, while further to the right are the "Forward" and "Backward" buttons (used to move the pickup ahead or back, track by track), index advance and retard buttons, and a pair of manual search buttons. Sound can be monitored while pressing the manual search buttons, even though the pickup is moving along the surface of the CD at several times its normal speed.

OUR LAB MEASUREMENTS

Frequency response for the CDP-302II was so uniform that there is no point in publishing a graph to show its response characteristics. Harmonic distortion measured just under Sony's specification, and even at the highest frequencies where most CD players exhibit considerably higher orders of distortion, our measurement of the CDP-302II was still remarkably low. The IM distortion figures were also impressive.

The signal-to-noise ratio was much better than Sony's specification, measuring at over 101 dB! Channel separation was also excellent. Reproduction of a 1 KHz square wave by the CDP-302II did not show any "ringing" (undulations) at the leading edge of the top of the waveform; such ringing is usually seen on CD players that use steep, multipole, analog output filters. This means the CDP-302II has excellent (flat) frequency response and no phase (time) delay.

ERROR CORRECTION AND TRACKING

We played a wide variety of program material (music) on this player, including the selections that are on our special error-correction/tracking disc. The "defective" tracks on this test disc played all the way through, without ever muting or mistracking. This means that the player easily corrected for missing information that extended over a length of more than 900 microns.

Furthermore, the CD player was about as impervious to external shock as any unit we have ever seen. We tapped the housing both on its top surface and on its sides, but its lightweight laser pickup never lost its place or mistracked.

Home CD Player Reviews

SUMMARY

When you first load a disc into this CD player, the display first tells you the total number of tracks and the total playing time of that disc. Programming is a bit tedious in that you have to advance the track numbers, one by one (instead of punching them in on a numeric keypad, as is the case with some other programmable players). However, once you get used to this method, it really doesn't take much longer than using a directly assignable numeric keypad.

This CD player passed all of our error-correction and tracking tests with flying colors. Of course, these tests don't tell you anything about how the CD player reproduces music; rest assured that the CDP-302II sounds every bit as good as it measures. If you find that you don't like the sounds produced by a CD played on this machine, blame the software (the disc itself) and not the player.

Some of our earliest CDs—those that we were convinced had been badly recorded—actually took on an acceptable musicality and better overall tonal balance when played on the Sony CDP-302II. It's hard to say whether the better sound results from Sony's switch to digital filtration and oversampling, or if its due to other circuit improvements.

However, we are glad Sony, one of the codevelopers of the CD format, joined other manufacturers (including the other codeveloper, Philips) in championing the digital filter plus oversampling approach to CD playback. In so doing, they have come up with a unit that retains all the mechanical superiority of earlier Sony CD players while providing what has to be one of the best sounding CD players, and offering it at a price that's hard to beat.

DENON DCD-1500

Denon America, Inc.

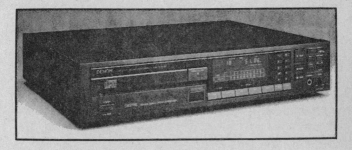

MANUFACTURER'S SPECIFICATIONS:

Frequency Response: 5 Hz to 20 KHz, ±0.3 dB.
Signal-to-Noise Ratio: 96 dB.
Dynamic Range: 96 dB.
Total Harmonic Distortion: Less than 0.0025%.
Channel Separation: 95 dB.
Number of Programmable Events: 20.
Audio Output Level: Fixed, 2.0 volts rms.
Dimensions: 17½ Wide x 3½ High x 14 inches Deep.
Approximate Retail Price: $580.
Approximate Low Price: $539.

While most CD players sound surprisingly similar, the DCD-1500 delivers slightly superior sound. In addition, it's easy to operate either from its full-featured wireless remote control or from the front panel, which has a display that shows all you need to know. You can also program up to 20 selections or several repeat-play modes. However, the advantage of the DCD-1500 stems more from its circuitry and sonic performance than from its other features.

CONTROL PANEL LAYOUT

Press the "Open/Close" button on the slide-out drawer at the upper left of the front panel to load or remove a CD. Below it is the power button, and to the right of the drawer glows the large, easy-to-read display, which shows the track and index numbers, time elapsed or remaining time, whether a disc is loaded, and small numbers (1 through 20) for designating selected programming tracks. Below the display are two pairs of buttons for skipping forward or back one track, and for audible search in either direction.

When used with numbered buttons, the "Index" and "Program Direct" buttons let you select the tracks you wish to play, or up to 20 random tracks for sequential programmed play. Larger "Play," "Pause," and "Stop" buttons sit to the right of the numbered buttons. Farther to the right are buttons for activating the various repeat-play modes (track, entire program, or entire disc), recalling previously programmed information, clearing the memory, and altering the display from elapsed to remaining time. Also found here is a timer on/off switch that, when connected to an external timer, lets the CD player be turned on at a specified time and begin playing any selections you've programmed. A stereo headphone jack with a volume-level control occupies the lower right corner.

The rear panel of the Denon DCD-1500 includes the usual left- and right-output jacks, as well as a subcode output for future use with video graphics adapters, when they become available.

OUR LAB MEASUREMENTS

The remarkably flat frequency response of the Denon DCD-1500 lends to its sonic smoothness. Even at very high frequencies, the distortion remains impressively low while stereo separation is excellent, a characteristic not true of all CD players. This outstanding stereo separation indicates careful layout of the player's analog stages, as well as complete independence of the digital-to-analog conversion system for the left and right stereo channels. This also results in both channels being reproduced in perfect phase with each other.

The Denon DCD-1500 ranks with the Pioneer PD-9010X and Sony CDP-620ESII in terms of the total elimination of unwanted sound beyond the audible range, which can ultimately affect what you hear. Background noise was virtually absent, with a signal-to-noise ratio better than that claimed by Denon, and output linearity that was excellent. The only minor discrepancy was that dynamic range measured slightly less than Denon listed. IM (intermodulation) distortion was extraordinarily low, while another form of IM distortion (CCIF-IM) was the lowest measured of any CD player we tested.

ERROR CORRECTION AND TRACKING

The Denon DCD-1500 matched our expectations in playing through the defects test disc without any skipping or muting. In fact, it played through the maximum width of the opaque wedge, the largest diameter of the dust simulation, and the simulated fingerprint smudge without so much as a hint of anything amiss. It also successfully tracked a damaged CD kept around for rigorous testing—a disc that has foiled more than one CD player in the past.

SUMMARY

To our listening panel, the DCD-1500 sounded a bit better than several CD players whose measurements weren't quite as good as those of this player. Ultimately, there seems to be some correlation between measurements and sound quality, providing the appropriate measurements are considered. Happily, this held true in the case of the Denon DCD-1500. It not only performed well in the lab tests and was easy to use, but it sounded as good as any CD player we tested. At its suggested retail price of $580, the Denon DCD-1500 is an excellent value.

dbx DX3

dbx, Inc.

MANUFACTURER'S SPECIFICATIONS:

Frequency Response (Without dbx Processing): 10 Hz to 20 KHz, +0.5 dB, -1.0 dB.

Signal-to-Noise Ratio (Without dbx Processing): 90 dB to 100 dB, depending on testing method.

Dynamic Range (With/Without dbx Processing): 60 to 106 dB/96 dB.

Total Harmonic Distortion (With/Without dbx Processing): 0.07%/0.002%.

Channel Separation (Without dbx Processing): 90 dB.

Number of Programmable Events: 9.

Audio Output Level: Fixed, 2.0 volts.

Dimensions: 17⅛ Wide x 3 ¹¹/₁₆ High x 11 ⁷/₁₆ inches Deep.

Approximate Retail Price: $599.

Approximate Low Price: $519.

If you think that all CD players are alike, consider the triple-beam DX3 from dbx, the company that developed the linear-companding noise reduction found on home cassette decks, professional compressors and expanders, and other consumer and professional signal-processing hardware. It was only natural that when dbx decided to enter the CD player market, they would add a little of their own signal-processing magic to their first CD unit, and so they did.

Following a pattern set by Bob Carver, whose somewhat higher priced CD player has also been selected for inclusion in this publication, the designers of the DX3 decided that they would let you, the user, "correct" some of the alleged "flaws" inherent in some recorded CDs. So, while Carver offers a couple of "fixes" that must be used together, or not at all, dbx offers no fewer than three sonic embellishments, each of which can be varied in degree or intensity.

DAIR, which stands for Digital Audio Impact Recovery, is a form of dynamic range expander that adds impact to musical transients. Why would anyone want even more dynamic range than is already available in CDs? According to dbx, some CDs made from old analog master tapes don't offer as much dynamic range as they should, and DAIR is supposed to correct for the failings of those particular CDs.

However, turning the DAIR control in the opposite direction invokes a variable amount of compression. This reduces the dynamic range of CDs when listening to them as "background music" or when recording cassettes from CDs to be played in your car.

If you have heard a CD in a car CD player, you will appreciate the ability to apply some compression to such recordings, albeit via a cassette copy of the original CD. When you play CDs in a car, the road and other ambient noises don't let you hear the soft musical passages when the volume is adjusted so the loud crescendos aren't blasting. Compression would enable you to adjust the volume so you can hear the soft parts of the music, without hurting your ears during the loud volumes. Ideally, dbx should license its circuit for use in car CD players.

A second control on the front panel of the DX3, labeled "Ambience," can be used to increase the apparent separation, or stereo "spread." Turned in the opposite direction, this control has the reverse effect, decreasing separation until the program material (music) sounds almost monophonic.

These last two sonic "tricks" are not new. The apparent increase in separation is accomplished by adding a bit of an out-of-phase left-channel signal to the right-channel output, along with a little of an out-of-phase right-channel signal to the left-channel output. In the case of the DX3, the cross-blending of out-of-phase signals is performed only for the middle and high frequencies.

Conversely, if you feel that a recording has been "spread out" too far or seems to have a "hole in the middle," turning the Ambience control in the opposite direction "tightens" the stereo image. Simply adding midrange to the signals (in-phase cross-blending of middle and high frequencies) accomplishes this reduced separation. As on the Carver CD player, the dbx DX3 has a switch that removes all of this special circuitry from the signal path. After all, some CDs do not require compression, expansion, stereo enhancement, or image "tightening."

As for the more usual features, the DX3 can be programmed to play up to nine tracks in any order. It can also repeat an entire CD, or the tracks you programmed, over and over again. "Skip" and "Scan" buttons let you move quickly from track to track, or while playing a CD with the sound at a reduced level, reach a specific point in a track rapidly. Although direct access to index points on a CD is not possible (there is no numeric keypad), the index numbers (if encoded on the CD) are displayed, so that you can stop the scan when you reach a desired index point in a given track, and then play from that point.

The display area shows the track number or elapsed time, or when the CD is not playing, a push of a button will indicate the total disc time. Three rows of indicator lights (LEDs) let you know how much and what type of signal processing is going on when either the DAIR or Compression mode are in use.

ADDITIONAL FRONT-PANEL CONTROLS

Besides the signal-processing controls described above, the front panel has the usual buttons, such as "Open/Close" for the front-loading disc drawer, "Stop/Pause," "Play," a pair of "Skip" buttons, two "Scan" buttons, "Repeat," "Program," "Display Mode" (for changing the display), and at the extreme left of the panel, a "Power" on/off button. No remote control is provided for the DX3. The usual output jacks are found at the rear of the player; however, there is no provision for controlling the output level and the DX3 does not have a headphone jack.

OUR LAB MEASUREMENTS

The frequency response was essentially flat from 20 Hz to 20 KHz, with a slight rise at about 15 KHz. At 20 KHz, response was down about 1 dB in each channel. The signal-to-noise ratio was very good, and total harmonic distortion was reasonably low.

However, the linearity was not nearly as good as we have measured for most other CD players. Signals that should have been reproduced at -80 dB from our test disc were actually -68.4 dB. This would be expected when using the compression circuits, but these results were obtained when these circuits were completely bypassed. With maximum compression, signals between the maximum recorded level and the -24 dB level changed by only 2.5 dB, while at -60 dB, the output signals were at -30 dB. Using somewhat less compression, the dynamic range was restored to a reasonable amount; enough so you could record onto cassettes without saturating the tapes, but not so little as to destroy the musical integrity.

IM distortion measured about average for CD players. Stereo separation for the DX3 was nowhere near the 90 dB claimed by dbx, and poor in comparison to most other players. Again, these measurements were made with the signal-processing circuits turned off. We suspect that even with these circuits disabled, signals must pass through certain integrated circuits that may have an effect on stereo separation. When the Ambience control is used, separation drops down to next to nothing, but that's what it's supposed to do in order to reduce the stereo spread.

Reproduction of a 1 KHz square wave by the DX3 was typical of that produced by CD players that employ steep, digital filters and two-times oversampling. The owner's manual states that a "third-order" analog filter is used after digital-to-analog conversion to gently attenuate frequencies above 20 KHz. Such minimal filtering is enough to get rid of any unwanted 88.2 KHz components, as well as sidebands of that frequency that result from the recovered music.

ERROR CORRECTION AND TRACKING

Not only was the DX3 able to play through our simulated scratches, the 800-micron-diameter simulated dust particles, and the simulated fingerprint smudge, but its resistance to vibration and shocks applied to its top surface were excellent.

SUMMARY

After we were satisfied that the player sounded good without any of the special signal-processing circuits, we pushed the button marked "In," which is located near the two rotary controls that determine the amounts of signal processing desired. Then we operated the "Dynamics" control, which offers either compression or further expansion, depending on which way you turn the knob. This signal-processing scheme "bats only .500"; the compression feature can be very useful, but the expansion part will rarely, or never, be put to use. You are not likely to find a single CD that can benefit from the DAIR expansion.

On the other hand, the compression half of this control merits appreciation. If you have ever tried to record CDs onto cassettes, and invariably ended up with either distorted musical crescendos or a noisy background (because you held down the recording levels so as not to saturate the tape during peaks), you will surely appreciate the action of this circuit.

We feel much more kindly disposed toward the Ambience control. If your CDs suffer from a lack of stereo "spread" or depth, or they exhibit exaggerated stereo effects, this control will help. While both of these effects are the result of improper microphone placement, mix-down, or final mastering, being able to compensate for these problems is a desirable feature. The trick of adding out-of-phase information from opposite channel signals is an old one, but it is very effective if used in moderation. Cross-blending has also been used before to reduce exaggerated stereo spread (and in FM, to reduce the noise generated during weak-signal stereo reception).

The nice thing about the DX3 is that you can regulate the amount of "blend" or stereo spread with precision, thanks to the continuously variable Ambience control. While Carver uses a similar out-of-phase stereo enhancement as part of his "Digital Time Lens" circuit, the amount of such enhancement is fixed. Therefore, you either have to take what he gives you or disable the circuit entirely by turning it off. Speaking of turning things off, dbx is to be complimented for having the good sense to provide an on/off switch for all of these "extras."

CARVER CD PLAYER

Carver Corp.

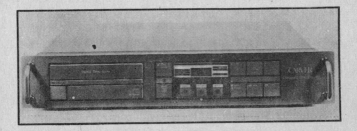

MANUFACTURER'S SPECIFICATIONS:

Frequency Response: 5 Hz to 20 KHz, ±0.5 dB.
Signal-to-Noise Ratio: 96 dB.
Dynamic Range: 96 dB.
Total Harmonic Distortion: 0.05% at 1 KHz.
Channel Separation: 86 dB.
Number of Programmable Events: 9.
Audio Output Level: Fixed, 1.9 volts at 0 dB.
Dimensions: 19 Wide x 3 7/16 High x 11¼ inches Deep.
Approximate Retail Price: $649.
Approximate Low Price: $614.

Audio engineer Bob Carver and his seven-year-old Carver Corporation have created some unusually named sonic innovations, such as "Charge-Coupled FM Detectors," "Magnetic Field Amplifiers," and "Sonic Holography." And now there's a "Digital Time Lens" in the company's first CD player. The Digital Time Lens lets you alter the tonal balance and stereo perspective of early, less-than-perfect CD recordings to make them sound more like their LP equivalents.

Carver developed the "Digital Time Lens," which is activated by a switch on the front panel of the Carver CD Player, after extensive comparison tests between early CDs and LP versions of the same recordings. He found there were two major differences between certain CDs and their LP counterparts.

The first has to do with stereo "depth" or separation. In a stereo program, the stereo effect is the difference between left and right signals (L-R), while the sum of these signals (L+R) conveys the mono (monophonic) information. Bob discovered that many CDs have less relative L-R information (compared to the quantity of L+R signal) than does the LP recording of the same program, at the same musical moment. In other words, the stereo information on the master tape (from which the original LP was produced) was compromised when the music was remixed for the CD. This was more common in early CD recordings than in more recent releases.

The second difference noted by Carver was, very simply, a difference in equalization, or overall frequency response. Carver observed a slight boost in the mid-bass and a slight reduction in the mid-treble on LPs when compared to CDs of the same album. Carver designed the Digital Time Lens circuitry to compensate for these effects at the flick of a switch.

In other words, if there wasn't enough L-R, this circuit formulated the missing component and added it to the sound. If a CD had overly bright mid-treble and somewhat diminished mid-bass, an equalization circuit (similar to a fixed tone control) smoothed out the response, or at least made it more similar to the LP version. Since many CDs won't benefit from these Digital Time Lens circuits, Carver wisely included a defeat switch that disables the circuitry.

CONTROL PANEL LAYOUT

Except for its exterior, the Carver CD player resembles other machines currently available. With a charcoal gray/black finish, it blends with other Carver products, and features a 19-inch-wide front panel equipped with handles. The subtle printing on the front panel is very subdued looking, though difficult to read in dim light.

The CD drawer at the panel's left side opens by touching a square pad to its right, and closes with another touch of that button or a tap on the drawer itself. The power on/off button lies below the disc drawer. A button under the open/close pad activates the Digital Time Lens, illuminating a light above it to confirm the circuit's operation.

Near the center of the panel, an alphanumeric display indicates the total number of tracks on a CD when you place it in the drawer; you can also have it display the total time on the disc. While the CD is playing, the display shows either the elapsed time in the track or the track number. During programming, this display prompts you to sequentially select tracks for P1 (program number 1), P2, and so on, up to P9, the maximum number of programs that can be "memorized" by the CD player's built-in microprocessor.

When the power is switched on, the laser pickup looks to see if a CD is in the drawer. If it doesn't find one, "dISC" flashes on the display until the drawer is opened; then "OPEn" is displayed. When you have finished programming or your program has been played, "End" is shown. Sitting under the display area are three small buttons labeled "Display" (for showing either the elapsed time or the track number), "Program" (for presetting tracks to be played), and "Repeat" (for programming the repetition of a CD or tracks that you had previously chosen).

Situated to the display's right side are six buttons that enable you to perform the following functions: play, fast forward and reverse that provide somewhat audible sound, track advance and reverse (one track at a time), and stop/pause. There is no headphone jack on this player.

OUR LAB MEASUREMENTS

Due to the Digital Time Lens, certain tests had to be repeated. For example, without using this circuitry, this CD player's usual frequency response was flat, varying less than 1 dB from 20 Hz to 20 KHz. When the Digital Time Lens pushbutton is depressed, however, the response exhibited a rise of nearly 2.5 dB at around 150 Hz, and decrease of between 2.0 and 2.5 dB at 3 KHz. This is the equalization compensation that Carver inserts to counteract the effects of poor CD recordings, as described earlier.

The already negligible harmonic distortion rose trivially at the limits of the bass and treble frequencies, while the output linearity remained precise down to very low levels. The signal-to-noise ratio was better with the Time Lens feature switched off, but it was somewhat poorer than the best players reviewed here. When the Time Lens was not in use, at mid-range frequencies, stereo separation was good, falling about 20 dB at very high frequencies.

ERROR CORRECTION AND TRACKING

The Carver CD Player ignored dropouts as wide as 800 microns, but it couldn't track the greatest width (900 microns) of the opaque wedge on our defects test disc. External shocks and the simulated fingerprint smudge and dust spots (up to 800 microns in diameter) also presented no difficulties. Although some newer CD players can deal with all of the defects on this special disc, the Carver unit will not present any tracking problems unless you are not careful with your discs or you purchase one with a major defect.

SUMMARY

Conducting listening tests on the Carver CD Player involved two sets of experiments. First, we auditioned some of our best Compact Discs without using the Digital Time Lens feature. Although satisfied with the results, we then turned on the Digital Time Lens Feature and—just as quickly—turned it off again. It just wasn't "right" for well-recorded discs; it gave them a rather dull treble and an exaggerated left-right sense of stereo separation.

Next, we selected some of the earliest CDs in our collection—specifically those that were originally disappointing. Depressing the Digital Time Lens button while listening to these discs really worked wonders. Suddenly, tonal balance seemed more correct and less strident, and what seemed like a flat stereo effect appeared to "open up" to some degree, affording the three-dimensional perspective that the musical performances demanded.

The Carver CD Player is an excellent unit that provides a feature you won't find on other machines. While most CDs probably won't benefit from it, a few early ones may. Fortunately, this CD player has many other features that make it worth considering.

BANG & OLUFSEN CDX

Bang & Olufsen of America, Inc.

MANUFACTURER'S SPECIFICATIONS:

Frequency Response: 3 Hz to 20 KHz, ±0.3 dB.
Signal-to-Noise Ratio: More than 96 dB.
Dynamic Range: More than 96 dB.
Total Harmonic Distortion: 0.003% at 0 dB level; 0.03% at -20 dB level.
Channel Separation: Greater than 94 dB, 20 Hz to 20 KHz.
Number of Programmable Events: 40.
Audio Output Level: 2.0 volts rms for 0 dB level.
Dimensions: 16½ Wide x 3 High x 12¼ inches Deep.
Approximate Retail Price: $699.
Approximate Low Price: $625.

Prices may vary; call local stores and check current ads.

The Danish firm of Bang & Olufsen is well known for the Scandinavian styling of its audio components. Many B & O models are on permanent exhibit at New York's Museum of Modern Art as an example of superb industrial design. B & O's elegantly styled CD player, their first such unit, matches their other components, but its design goes beyond aesthetics.

While the beautiful CDX is sure to be a conversation piece in any home, it is also one of the easiest CD players to use. Its gently sloping, black-tinted, semitransparent plastic control surface bears words and numerals that need only to be lightly touched to initiate action. No switches, knobs, or other protrusions deface the top of this unit. The CDX compensates for its lack of remote control by offering random access to specific tracks along with ample programmability. You can program up to 40 commands for a given CD, but since few discs contain that many tracks, you can repeat several tracks.

CONTROL PANEL LAYOUT

"Control" is actually a misnomer here. No operating controls adorn this unit in the traditional sense, other than an "Eject" button at the left of the narrow front surface of the unit and a "Play" button at the far right. To install a disc, you simply press "Eject" after first turning on the unit by touching "Play." If a CD is already in place when you press "Play," the disc will be scanned and the total number of tracks (up to 20) will be displayed by illuminated green numerals on the control surface.

At that point you have several options. Simply touching "Play" allows the CD to be played from beginning to end. Or you can program up to 40 tracks to be played in any order, using the 0 through 9 white numerals that appear below the green ones. Again, all you need is a light finger touch above the selected number, followed by another light touch of "Store," which appears to the right of the numerals.

If you want to hear most, but not all, of the tracks, Bang & Olufsen simplifies that task, too. After touching the number of the unwanted track, you simply touch "Clear" to eliminate that track from the playing sequence. For a disc that has many tracks, omitting one track is much easier and faster than having to store, say, 19 out of 20 tracks.

If a disc is not already in place when you press the "Play" button, a red question mark appears in the main display area to the right of the track and programming numerals. At that point, pressing "Eject" raises three quarters of the top of the unit, giving access to the CD "turntable." At the same time, the turntable itself tilts up toward you, almost as if inviting you to place a CD on it. Once a disc is in place, gently touching the open lid causes it to close as quietly and smoothly as it opened. Alternatively, you can touch "Play" on what B & O calls their "Sensi-touch" panel, and the lid will close; play will then start from the beginning of the disc.

The major, red LED display serves four purposes. Initially, it shows the elapsed time of the track that is playing. If you touch "Display," which is near the actual display area, you first see a readout of total elapsed time from the beginning of the disc. Touch this word again, and the display shows the track and index number currently being played. Finally, a question mark symbol in the display tells you that you have done something wrong, and that the CDX cannot follow your command. Loading a CD upside down, for example, or asking for tracks that do not exist will result in the question mark display.

Fast forward and fast reverse are accomplished by touching appropriate words on the Sensi-touch surface; you cannot hear the music while using these modes. Touching "Return" allows backward movement, track by track, should you want to hear an earlier track on a disc, while lightly pressing "Advance" skips tracks in the forward direction. Touching "Repeat" allows you to repeat the playing of a CD up to four times. Briefly touching the word "Stop" pauses the playing of the CD; it can be resumed from the same spot on the disc by touching "Play." However, holding your finger on "Stop" for more than two seconds suspends playing completely and the disc stops spinning.

OUR LAB MEASUREMENTS

Frequency response of the CDX CD player was flat within one quarter of a decibel from 20 Hz to 20 KHz. Since Bang & Olufsen uses the same D/A conversion technique employed by Philips (i.e., four-times oversampling and 14-bit linear conversion), steep output filters are not required; more gentle analog filters can be used to minimize phase shift.

Total harmonic distortion (THD) matched Bang & Olufsen's specifications, while the signal-to-noise ratio far exceeded the company's claims. Channel separation was also very good; it decreased only slightly at the highest frequencies.

A 1 KHz square wave reproduced by this CD player corresponded exactly to the results obtained for other machines that use this type of digital filtering and oversampling. Reproduction of a unit pulse was also typical of the results obtained with other players employing this same kind of D/A conversion.

ERROR CORRECTION AND TRACKING

Tracking of this unit was not quite as good as that of some other recently tested third-generation CD players. Specifically, the error-correction circuitry and servo-tracking arrangement was unable to get through our "obstacle course" defects disc. We heard a "glitch" while playing the track covered with the 900-micron-wide opaque area. Admittedly, that's the widest opaque area on the test disc, but several recent CD players have been able to get through it without any audible problems.

In all fairness to B & O, we must add that their CD player played right through the simulated dust particles and fingerprint smudge on the same disc.

SUMMARY

From the logical and easy-to-understand layout of the brief owner's manual to the easy-to-operate CDX itself, this product is a typical Bang & Olufsen masterpiece. We just don't know how much of the internal workings of this unit are built by B & O and how much of it comes from other sources. We suspect that the D/A conversion circuitry and related parts (or at least the D/A chips) come from Philips, while the transport mechanism, with its unique lift-up disc platter, probably originated at B & O.

We had no complaints about the sound quality of this unit. In all respects, the sound reproduction was reminiscent of that generated by the Philips (Magnavox brand) CD players we tested, all of which use the same approach to digital-to-analog conversion. That is, there was none of the harshness attributed to machines that use a 44.1 KHz sampling rate with steep, multipole analog filters at their outputs.

The price of the CDX, in our opinion, is quite reasonable considering its many operating features, the ease with which it executes those features, and the attempt to simplify the way people interact with machines (via human engineering, or ergonomics) that has almost become synonymous with the Danish styling of Bang & Olufsen's components.

SONY CDP-620ESII

Sony Corp. of America

MANUFACTURER'S SPECIFICATIONS:

Frequency Response: 2 Hz to 20 KHz, ±0.3 dB.
Signal-to-Noise Ratio: 96 dB.
Dynamic Range: 96 dB.
Total Harmonic Distortion: Less than 0.0025% at 1 KHz.
Channel Separation: Greater than 95 dB.
Number of Programmable Events: 20.
Audio Output Level: Fixed, 2.0 volts rms for 0 dB level; variable, 0.05 to 2.0 volts rms.
Dimensions: 17 Wide x 3¼ High x 14¼ inches Deep.

Approximate Retail Price: $950.
Approximate Low Price: $914.

The CDP-620ESII shares many aspects of Sony's top-of-the-line (and most expensive) CD player, the CDP-650ESD. The biggest difference between these two models is their price; the CDP-620ESII carries a suggested retail price of $950, while the list price of the CDP-650ESD is $1,300.

You sacrifice little to save $350. The 620ESII omits the unique digital-code output port on the rear panel of the 650ESD. Don't confuse this digital output with the special accessory connector that will be needed for attaching a video graphics interface box when it becomes available; both the 650ESD and the 620ESII have that connector. The additional output port on the 650ESD allows you to access the audio bit (binary digit) stream itself, allowing digital-to-digital audio data transfer.

Another difference between the two units is a headphone output jack found on the 620ESII, which is missing from the higher priced 650ESD. Sony says that using a headphone amplifier in the circuitry of a "pure" CD player, such as the 650ESD, can affect the sound quality. Sony apparently regards the lower priced 620ESII as a CD player in which total perfection is not the goal, permitting the minor compromise of integrating a headphone amplifier and its associated output jack. We welcomed the addition of the jack on the lower cost unit; if it introduced any sound degradation, we failed to hear it!

CONTROL PANEL LAYOUT

The front panel of the CDP-620ESII is almost identical to that of the more expensive CDP-650ESD. The disc drawer remains pretty much as it has been on earlier

Sony home CD players, sitting on the panel's left side and opened by pressing an "Open/Close" button to its right. It closes by touching the drawer front, the "Open/Close" key again, or the "Play" button, which also initiates disc play.

Numbered keys from 1 to 20, plus a key labeled "+10," are found near the center of the panel. They are used to call up desired tracks for play or for random-access programming. The "+10" button speeds up the process if you need to access a track number above 20. Track 44, for example (if one existed on the CD), would be called up by touching the "+10" button four times, and then pressing the "4" button.

The "Play," "Pause," "AMS" (Automatic Music Search, for track advance and track retard), and play-mode keys ("Continue," "Single," and "Program") are found to the right of the numeric keyboard. Below the keyboard are the "Check" and "Clear" keys used to verify programmed instructions or clear them from memory. A "Stop" key and two manual search keys are near the lower right corner of the panel. The search keys provide fast access to a given point on a CD, in either direction, while listening to the disc.

At the panel's lower left corner are switches that turn the player on and off manually, or by means of an optional external timer. Additional buttons beneath the display area are "Repeat" (for playing part of a disc between two preselected points over and over again), "A to B" (for setting those starting and ending points), "Time" (for toggling between elapsed time and remaining time that is shown on the display), "Auto Delay," and "Shuffle Play."

When the "Auto Delay" button is depressed, two seconds of blank space are inserted before the player begins to play the first selection. This function can be turned off by pressing the same button a second time. The interesting "Shuffle Play" feature plays all of the selections on a disc shuffled (like a deck of playing cards) in random order. When the entire disc has been played once, the shuffle play automatically cancels itself. There seems to be no end as to what you can do with a CD player that has a computer chip.

The front panel's display area presents a wide variety of useful data. "Disc" illuminates when a CD has been inserted in the drawer. A track indicator briefly displays the total number of tracks on the disc, followed by the actual track number being played. Elapsed time of track play is also shown after first revealing the total time on the disc. Remaining time can be toggled with elapsed time.

Also in the display area is a "PGM" (ProGraM) indicator that lights up when the player is in the standby mode for programmed play. "Index" shows the index number of the selection being played. If the disc lacks index segments, "Index" displays "1" at all times. A numeric grid (0 through 18) shows how many selections you have programmed, as well as the one currently being played. If you program more than 18 choices, "Over" lights up to denote that fact. A headphone jack on the left and a volume control at the lower right of the panel completes the layout.

A full-function, wireless remote-control unit, which Sony calls a "Remote Commander," duplicates nearly every function that can be activated at the CD player's front panel, including random-access programming, all of the repeat-play features, shuffle play, and even remote adjustment of the level coming from the variable output jacks.

The rear panel of the 620ESII has fixed and variable-level output jacks, plus a multiple-pin connector intended for future use with the graphics and video interface adapter referred to earlier. The rear panel also has a "Play Mode" initializing switch that sets this mode for either continuous, single-selection, or programmed play.

OUR LAB MEASUREMENTS

Frequency response varied by no more than one tenth of a decibel over the entire range of 20 Hz to 20,000 Hz, better than both Sony's specifications and one of the best units tested. Harmonic distortion measured only slightly less than the published specifications. The signal-to-noise ratio measured exactly as claimed, while using a common adjustment factor (A-weighting) increased the S/N reading to exactly 100 dB. IM distortion measured pleasingly low, and stereo separation was quite good.

Reproduction of a 1 KHz square wave by this new Sony CD player was identical to that obtained from the CDP-650ESD. Specifically, the shape of the square wave was indicative of digital filtering combined with two-times oversampling, which is the method used by most late-model CD players. Reproduction of the pulse signal was also identical to that obtained from the Sony CDP-650ESD and other recent CD players.

ERROR CORRECTION AND TRACKING

A lower-mass pickup and a linear-motor pickup drive designed for the third-generation Sony CD players have been used in the 620ESII with superb results, both in terms of searching speed and tracking stability that showed a lack of susceptibility to external shock and vibration. This means that the defects test disc employed to evaluate error-correction and tracking ability posed no real challenge for the Sony CDP-620ESII.

SUMMARY

When Sony says this CD player can access any point on a CD in one second, they're not exaggerating. Several times, using test discs that have a large number of tracks, we instructed the machine to search for double-digit numbered (ten or greater) tracks. Almost before we could look up from the remote-control unit on which we had entered those instructions, music from the requested track began to play.

Of course, the truly important characteristic of this or any other CD player is the sound quality it provides. We have maintained that the best sound we ever heard from any CD player came from the Sony CDP-650ESD. We can't say that the sound of the CDP-620ESII surpasses that of the CDP-650ESD, but we can tell you that after hours of listening comparisons, our experts could not detect any difference in sound quality between the two players.

That being the case, there would seem to be little, if any, reason to buy the expensive CDP-650ESD, even if money is no object and perfection is your goal. Unless you have some special reason for wanting a separate digital-code output on your CD player, the CDP-620ESII should do as well as Sony's more expensive model, the CDP-650ESD.

REVOX B225

Studer Revox America, Inc.

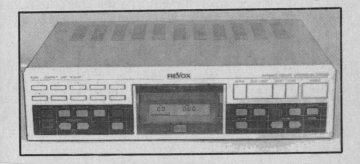

MANUFACTURER'S SPECIFICATIONS:

Frequency Response: 20 Hz to 20 KHz, +0 dB, -0.6 dB, phase-linear.

Signal-to-Noise Ratio (Weighted): Greater than 100 dB (20 Hz to 20 KHz).

Signal-to-Noise Ratio (Linear): Greater than 96 dB (20 Hz to 20 KHz).

Dynamic Range: 96 dB.

Total Harmonic Distortion: Less than 0.006% (20 Hz to 20 KHz).

Channel Separation: Greater than 90 dB (20 Hz to 20 KHz).

Number of Programmable Events: 19.

Audio Output Level: Fixed, 2.0 volts rms; variable, 0 to 2.0 volts rms.

Dimensions: 17¾ Wide x 4¼ High x 13 inches Deep.

Approximate Retail Price: $1,150.

Approximate Low Price: $1,094.

It comes as no surprise that this CD player, the first from Studer Revox, is one of the most sophisticated, rugged, yet easy-to-use units that we have ever tested. After all, many broadcast and recording studios throughout the world insist on Studer tape equipment, while other audiophiles believe that Revox products (the brand name used on consumer merchandise designed and developed by the Studer organization) have the same attributes as the company's professional electronic components.

However, we were surprised by the B225's retail price. We expected this Revox CD player to be among the world's most expensive, as well as among the best units available. While it certainly lived up to the latter expectation, it is priced no higher than some of the first generation CD players that offered only a fraction of the versatility and sound quality.

Studer Revox completely designed the software responsible for the elaborate programming sequences that can be processed by the B225. Programming extends to as many as 20 individual steps (counting the mode in which you begin), and it can include all of the following possibilities, used individually or in combination with each other:

1. Reprogramming of a given play sequence.

2. Programming of CD segments based on time boundaries within a given track number.

3. Programming with "mixed boundaries"; that is, the starting point can be the beginning of a track number, while the ending point can be specified as a time in minutes and seconds.

4. Programs can be modified in a simple manner. Each entry within the program steps can be altered individually.

5. Writing a new program sequence overrides the old one. It is not necessary to cancel the old program before entering a new one.

6. A loop command can be entered as the last step of a program. This will cause the entire program to be repeated until the "Stop" control is used.

7. It is possible to include a "pause" or "stop" in the programming sequence. When this is done, the CD player switches into the "Pause" or "Stop" mode after the appropriate step has been executed. The program resumes by depressing the "Pause" button when you are ready to continue listening.

8. If a pause is desired after each step of the program, a special "Autostop" key can be depressed before the start of the program. This will activate the "Pause" function after each step.

9. Sometimes it may be useful to audibly signal the end of a long program or a sequence within a program. This can be done by programming the sounding of a "Calibration Tone," which will remain audible until it is disabled at the front panel.

10. You can even enter a command in your program to turn off the electrical power to the CD player.

CONTROL PANEL LAYOUT

The first thing we noticed about the B225 was the logical layout of its front panel. A multifunctional display is dead-center on the panel, situated on the front of the disc drawer, while controls and buttons for program selection and memorization are grouped together at the left end of the front panel. Located at the right third of the panel are special controls, such as volume (for the variable-level output jacks) and a stereo headphone output jack.

Also at the right end of the panel are frequently used controls, such as "Power," "Load" (for opening and closing the drawer), "Stop," "Repeat," and "Play/Next." This last key initiates play from the stop mode and, if already in the play mode, advances play to the next track (or in the case of programmed play, to the next programmed step).

Below this row of commonly used controls are the "Autostop" button, "Fast Forward" and "Fast Reverse" keys, the "Pause" key, and a button labeled "Display" that can indicate the elapsed time of the selection currently being played, elapsed time from the start of the disc, or the current time into the track that is playing. Other features and touch buttons along the lower right of the panel include a "Calibration Tone," "Volume Increase" and "Volume Decrease," and a stereo headphone output jack. The "Calibration Tone" button sends a 1,000 Hz tone to the outputs; the amplitude of this tone corresponds to maximum possible output level from a CD. This tone can, therefore, be used to set the recording level controls on a tape recorder, since the maximum level, in the case of digital Compact Discs, is fixed by the CD system and will never be exceeded. You can set recording levels with confidence using this test tone.

The display area of the B225 offers a wealth of information. In the normal (nonprogrammed) mode, it shows track and index number, time from the beginning of the current track (or, from the start of the disc), and whether the Pause, Autostop, or Loop modes have been activated. It also displays, in a series of horizontal, illuminated bars, the total number of selections on the CD, how many of these have been played, and the quantity still to be played.

In the program mode, the display's information changes. The word "Step" with a number below it indicates the program play mode and that you are executing the program step denoted by the displayed number. The next field of the display shows the current track being played, while to the right, the display shows the final position of the programmed step (if an end point has been specified) or it displays the next, upcoming track called for in the programming steps. The horizontal bars below the major display continue to indicate the same information as they did in the normal play mode.

Numeric keys ("0" through "9") sit at the upper left of the panel, and are used for direct access to a given track or for programming. Below these keys are the following controls: a "Store" button; a "Mark" button for setting a starting and stopping mark in the programming mode while a selection is playing; a "Track/Time" switch for varying the display from track to real-time indications; a "Cursor" key that moves a cursor (pointer) around the display for setting up desired times, and so on; and a "Program" key that sets up the player for program entry mode.

A "Loop" button along the bottom right of this panel section repeats the CD or the program until you press the "Stop" button. Two other buttons in this area let you "page" through your previously entered program instructions, in either direction. This is useful if you want to edit or alter your program.

A sensor at the lower left of the panel detects the infrared signals emitted by Revox's remote-control unit, which also works with their other components. When used with this CD player, the remote-control unit (Revox Model B201) lets you execute major operating functions, such as entering (keying in) the desired tracks in the normal playing mode, "Play," "Stop," "Fast Forward," "Fast Reverse," and "Pause."

Reading about all these controls may be intimidating. However, once you start using this magnificent product, programming comes easy. The reason for this is that the panel is well laid out, and the controls are succinctly and clearly labeled.

OUR LAB MEASUREMENTS

As has been our experience with other Revox products, published specifications were unusually conservative. Frequency response for the Revox B225 was extremely flat, deviating less than one quarter of a decibel from 20 Hz to 20 KHz. Total harmonic distortion for maximum output matched, or was lower than, Revox's claims, while the signal-to-noise ratio measured better than their specifications. Intermodulation distortion was impressively low, while linearity was extremely accurate down to -80 dB. Stereo separation remained quite high at all frequencies.

Reproduction of a 1 KHz, digitally generated square wave signal was typical of that obtained from players using digital filtering before D/A (digital-to-analog) conversion. Note that the B225 uses two independent D/A conversion circuits, so there is no time delay, or phase differential, between left-channel and right-channel information.

ERROR CORRECTION AND TRACKING

The Revox B225 had no trouble playing through (and ignoring) all of the defects built into our Philips test disc. That means it was able to correct for dropouts extending to 900 microns in length, 900-micron simulated dust or dirt spots, and a long, semiopaque, simulated fingerprint smudge. We were a bit more brutal than usual in our "tapping tests" along the sides and top of this rugged unit, and we still failed to cause any mistracking.

SUMMARY

If you are looking for a CD player that doesn't occupy very much space on your shelf or tabletop, this is probably not the unit for you. You can find other CD players that are much smaller in size and lighter in weight. However, if you want a CD player that is more versatile in its programming capabilities than just about any other unit available, seriously consider purchasing the Revox B225.

We expected sonic and mechanical perfection from Revox's first CD player, and we were rewarded. Sound quality was beyond reproach. In all of these test reports, we have stressed that there is little audible difference between CD players. Nevertheless, we felt the Revox B225 sounded "cleaner" than other units; instruments seemed better defined during ensemble playing and in orchestral works. Stereo imaging was magnificent on some of the newer CDs.

In addition, the ease with which complex programming could be performed seemed like a fitting accompaniment to the high technology involved in the actual playing and tracking of CDs.

All in all, the Revox B225 is a superb CD player. We can't think of a single feature or control that we would have arranged differently.

SHURE D5000

Shure Brothers Inc.

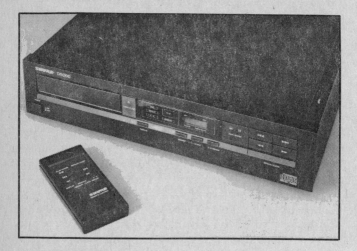

MANUFACTURER'S SPECIFICATIONS:

Frequency Response: 5 Hz to 20 KHz, ±0.3 dB.
Signal-to-Noise Ratio: 100 dB.
Dynamic Range: 93 dB.
Total Harmonic Distortion: 0.006% at 1 KHz, 0.007% at
   20 KHz.
Channel Separation: 85 dB at 1 KHz.
Number of Programmable Events: 15.
Audio Output Level: 2.0 volts rms maximum.
Dimensions: 16.9 Wide x 3.9 High x 10 inches Deep.
Approximate Retail Price: $399.
Approximate Low Price: $399.

Shure Brothers, best known for their superb phonograph cartridges, microphones, and professional audio products, has released their first CD player, the competitively priced D5000. It features wireless remote control and 15-track random programmability with access to as many as 99 tracks. Unfortunately, you can't access index points on CDs. Other convenience features include a two-speed audible scan and various repeat functions, including disc repeat, memory repeat, and musical phrase or section repeat.

The D5000 has a three-beam laser tracking system, which many manufacturers are adopting for more stable and accurate laser tracking. The D5000 incorporates 16-bit D/A processing and the smoothing effects of 2-to-1 oversampling. Digital filtering is employed in the pre-D/A stages, with additional analog filtering used ahead of the player's outputs.

CONTROL PANEL LAYOUT

The engineers who designed this unit obviously went to great pains to come up with a multiple-function control arrangement to keep the front panel of this CD player uncluttered and nonintimidating. On the whole, they have done a good job.

The power switch, disc drawer, and "Open/Close" button are at the panel's left end. Clustered at the right end of the panel are Random Program Select/Track Skip buttons, fast-forward and fast-reverse buttons for audibly finding a desired point on a disc, and a "Pause/Play" button. Only after reading the owner's manual very carefully did we discover that this last button also serves as a "Stop" button—providing you hold it down for more than two seconds. A long bar-like pushbutton below these major controls is used to activate repeat-play of an entire disc or, when pushed again, to end the repeat-play mode.

A display area near the center of the panel shows either the elapsed time from the beginning of the track that is currently playing or, if switched to its alternate mode, the track and index number being played. Because you can't access a specific index number directly, we found it rather odd that Shure chose to display the index numbers. However, you can use the fast-forward and fast-reverse buttons, while you watch the display, to "zero in" on a given index point on a disc; this may take a little practice.

Also in this display area are illuminated words that indicate functions such as repeat playback, "A-to-B" phrase repeat, "Memory" playback of programmed tracks, and the presence or absence of a CD inside the disc drawer. Four small buttons below the display area are used in display selection, memory entry, memory clearing, and selection of "A" and "B" points when choosing the musical-phrase repeat function.

The ten buttons on the wireless remote-control unit duplicate the functions of the front panel's ten buttons. Neither the front panel nor the remote control has a numeric keypad, thus denying you direct access to tracks. To reach a specific track, either from the front panel or the remote control, you must hold down the track "skip" button to pass over the unwanted tracks. You can, however, program this CD player for random play from either the remote control or the front panel. The rear panel of the D5000 has a pair of output jacks.

OUR LAB MEASUREMENTS

Frequency response of the D5000 varied by less than one half of a decibel over the entire audio range (20 Hz to 20,000 Hz). Shure manages to maintain extremely close tolerances in their output analog-filter circuitry. The excellent signal-to-noise ratio was only a couple of decibels lower than the best we have measured for any CD player. Total harmonic distortion measured satisfactorily low, while IM distortion, although low, was slightly greater than some competing CD players.

Channel separation was typical of most CD players, gradually decreasing at higher frequencies. This decrease is generally attributed to coupling between channels in the final analog-audio output stages and wiring, rather than to the digital processing circuitry. Linearity of the D5000 was excellent all the way from 0 dB to -80 dB.

Short access time—the time required for the laser pickup to find the beginning of the next track while the current track is playing—measured just over 1 second. Long access time—the time required for the laser pickup to move from track 1 to track 99 on a special 99-track test disc—measured only 4 seconds; this is quite fast. These figures compare favorably to Shure's specification, which lists the average access time as 0 to 3 seconds.

ERROR CORRECTION AND TRACKING

Shure's D5000 played straight through our defects test disc without any evidence of mistracking, despite the presence of opaque, 900-micron sections. We also subjected the player to mild vibration and shock tests while a CD was playing, and found it to be among the best-sounding units when subjected to these tests.

SUMMARY

We listened to several of our favorite CDs on the Shure D5000, and we were very pleased with the sound quality of the reproduced music. Shure strikes a proper balance between the action of the digital filters and that of the analog filters. This results in a complete lack of any "graininess" or loud, harsh highs sometimes heard from other CD players.

The remote-control unit worked well over a wide enough angle and distance so that you won't have to sit in a precise position in the room to ensure its proper operation. When first depressed, the fast-forward/reverse and track advance/retard buttons work slowly, followed by an accelerated action when held down for more than a couple of seconds; this was just right for accessing specific points or tracks on a disc quickly and precisely.

We also liked the sequential action of the front-panel display, both when a disc is initially loaded, and during play or programmed play when the elapsed-time mode is selected. The track number is displayed automatically as the laser pickup assembly moves from one track to another, and then reverts to elapsed-time notation. We had not seen this nice innovation before in any CD player we tested.

Shure's entry into the CD player market and other state-of-the-art consumer audio products suggests that this experienced company is not about to rest on past achievements. Instead, it clearly means they intend to keep up with changing audio technology.

AKAI CD-A70

Akai America, Ltd.

MANUFACTURER'S SPECIFICATIONS:

Frequency Response: 5 Hz to 20 KHz, ±0.5 dB.
Signal-to-Noise Ratio: 95 dB.
Dynamic Range: 95 dB.
Total Harmonic Distortion: 0.003% at 1 KHz.
Channel Separation: 90 dB at 1 KHz.
Number of Programmable Events: 27 (see text).
Audio Output Level: 2.0 volts.
Dimensions: 17.3 Wide x 3.1 High x 10.2 inches Deep.
Approximate Retail Price: $475.
Approximate Low Price: $444.

After three generations of CD players, some manufacturers recognize the previously unaddressed finer points of CD reproduction. A good example of this is shown in Akai's top CD player, the CD-A70.

For instance, consider the matter of digital filtration. Almost all recently designed CD players employ digital filtering and oversampling, but not all digital filters are alike. Some provide out-of-band attenuations (reductions in unwanted, inaudible frequencies) of no more than 50 dB or so, while the high-performance digital filters employed in the Akai CD-A70 provide an attenuation of 90 dB.

The use of a three-beam laser is almost becoming standard practice these days, but the design of servo-control systems, which respond to deviations from perfect tracking, vary widely from unit to unit. Akai's servo-control system is particularly good at maintaining accurate tracking, even in the presence of substantial data dropouts. Their servo-control system is extremely well isolated and insulated from the effects of external resonance and vibration. The CD-A70 uses what Akai describes as "an anti-resonant composite new metal construction in the chassis cover." Furthermore, the entire pickup assembly and disc tray are free-floating, suspended from the main chassis by anti-resonant rubber pads, further isolating these parts from external vibration.

From the user's point of view, most of these improvements go unnoticed, although added together, they contribute to better sound reproduction. Improved error correction and tracking accuracy means that less data interpolation (estimation of missing data between two known values) is necessary, even when there are minor scratches or dust particles on the CD. That, in turn, means more accurate sound reproduction.

One appealing feature, which was even present on earlier Akai CD players, has to do with random programming on the CD-A70. While ten numeric keys are used for this function, Akai added what they call "Natural Logic Operation." Buttons labeled "And," "To," "Index," and "Without" let you enter instructions such as "1 To 5 And 7 To 10 Without 9." After such an entry, pressing the "Program Start" button will cause the machine to play tracks 1 through 5, followed by tracks 7, 8, and 10, skipping track 9.

Index points can also be programmed into the CD

player's memory, following the same sort of logical instructions. A total of 27 steps can be programmed in this manner, but because each step (or group of steps) may call up several tracks, the programming capacity is actually greater than exists in a more conventional type of programming sequence.

Search and play functions, such as Music Search, Index Search, Manual Search, A-B Repeat, and Program Skip, are also possible. Track selection, opening and closing of the disc tray, and other operations can be controlled from the supplied wireless remote control, as well as from the front panel.

Like so many other newer CD players, the CD-A70 includes a subcode output terminal for future use with discs that will contain data needed to create digital graphics (still pictures, text, etc.) when properly interfaced to your TV set or video monitor.

CONTROL PANEL LAYOUT

The disc drawer, power button, and headphone jack occupy the far left third of the front panel. A liquid crystal display (LCD) at the center of the panel shows the CD player's mode, total and individual elapsed time, track number, and index number. Besides showing when programming is in operation, the LCD includes indicators for the "And," "To," and "Without" functions described earlier. The type of repeat play you select is also shown on the display, as are indicators for "Play" and "Pause" modes.

Buttons for "Program Start/Pause," "A to B" repeat, "Clear" (program), and "Display" (for altering the display mode) are found to the right of the display area. Further to the right are the numeric keys for random programming, as well as the "logic" keys and a "Repeat" key. Clustered at the right end of the panel are the "Open/Close," "Play/Pause," "Stop," "Skip," and fast "Search" buttons. A slider control for adjusting the headphone output level (volume) sits at the panel's lower right.

OUR LAB MEASUREMENTS

The excellent frequency response varied less than two thirds of a decibel throughout the audible range. Signal-to-noise ratio was very good, approaching that shown by the best CD players. Linearity was accurate to within 0.1 dB from the maximum recorded level down to -60 dB, and within 1.8 dB down to -80 dB. IM distortion was also impressively low. Dynamic range measured 3 dB greater than claimed by Akai.

Although the measured total harmonic distortion slightly exceeded the manufacturer's specifications, its very low figure demonstrated the superiority of the digital filter design. While many players produce high levels of "beats" when high-frequency test tones are reproduced (often equivalent to several percent of distortion), only very minor levels of such beats were observed when measuring the distortion levels of this CD player. In this regard, the Akai CD-A70 is comparable to the very few CD players that we have measured and found to produce such low levels of out-of-band beat components.

Separation between channels measured close to 85 dB at mid-frequencies. Again, the attention to detail in designing the analog stages and the layout of the wiring in this unit is apparent when you look at the separation at high frequencies. For most CD players we have measured, separation figures fall off rapidly as you approach the high frequency end of the spectrum, often decreasing to 60 dB or less. While that's more than enough separation for excellent stereo imaging, or perspective, the fact that Akai was able to maintain separations of nearly 80 dB even at 20 KHz speaks well for other aspects of the layout and design of this unit.

ERROR CORRECTION AND TRACKING

With all the sophisticated servo-tracking systems and anti-resonance, vibration-resistant construction found in this CD player, we were not surprised to find that the CD-A70 managed to play through our defects disc without ever mistracking.

This machine was also particularly impervious to external vibration. Besides our usual finger-tapping tests on the sides and top of the unit, we mounted the entire CD player atop one of our reference speaker systems and turned up the volume until we felt a fair amount of vibration being transferred to the CD player itself. We detected no difference in sound quality compared to the way the same music sounded when the CD player was well isolated from any external vibration. We would hardly recommend mounting CD players on top of speakers, however, unless you want to conduct this type of experiment.

SUMMARY

If you believe that all CD players sound alike, we recommend that you check out the Akai CD-A70. Its refined digital filtering, carefully designed analog output stages, and resonance-resistant construction all contribute to the utterly clean and "grit-free" sound that we heard when playing some CDs we had previously blamed for such imperfections as a rather strident sounding high-end and less-than-perfect stereo imaging, or depth. Of course, some of the earliest CDs still suffer sonic flaws that not even this state-of-the-art player can "correct." However, given a reasonably well-recorded CD, the Akai CD-A70 delivers highly satisfying sound reproduction that is comparable to the best of the newer CD players.

As for the features not directly related to sound quality, we especially liked the "logical" programming system. It's easy to understand and use. However, there are a couple of ways in which you can upset the system. For example, if you tried to enter "1 To 3 Without 2 And 5 To 8 Without 6," the second "To" would not be accepted. It seems that the "Without" command must always be entered after the last "To." The "Index" command key must also always be used before the "Without" command. For instance, "1 And 2, Index 1 And 3" is an acceptable programming order, but "1 To 3 Without 2, Index 2" isn't; the system won't accept the "Index" command in the second example.

The Akai CD-A70 deserves to be classified as a true fourth-generation CD player, incorporating just about all of the improvements that manufacturers have learned about during the short history of home Compact Disc players. It's suggested retail price is more than justified in light of its excellent sonic and mechanical performance.

The following budget-priced CD players offer performance that is essentially similar to more expensive models, except without some of their subtleties and niceties. Since audible differences tend to be highly subjective, we cannot guarantee that these inexpensive CD players sound identical to those with higher price tags. All of the following CD players represent the newest generation of machines, and arrived too late for laboratory testing.

TECHNICS SL-P110

Technics

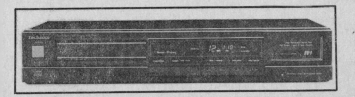

MANUFACTURER'S SPECIFICATIONS:

Frequency Response: 4 Hz to 20 KHz, ±0.5 dB.
Signal-to-Noise Ratio: More than 96 dB.
Dynamic Range: More than 92 dB.
Total Harmonic Distortion: 0.006% (1 KHz, 0 dB).
Channel Separation: More than 96 dB.
Number of Programmable Events: 20.
Audio Output Level: 2 volts at 0 dB.
Dimensions: 17 Wide x 3 High x 9.5 inches Deep.
Approximate Retail Price: $320.
Approximate Low Price: $294.

Technics wasted no time joining the CD revolution, immediately competing with the CD format's codevelopers, Sony and Philips, by releasing a machine that was mammoth when compared to the competition. Technics, a division of Matsushita, which also markets under the Panasonic, National, and Quasar names, so eagerly sought perfection of CD technology that it constructed an in-house CD pressing plant. While originally built to gain expertise about the CD format, the Technics pressing plant went on to gain fame as the contractor for Telarc's CDs, known for their remarkable clarity and sound quality.

Technics now sells its fourth generation of CD players at prices that were unthinkable just two years ago. Representing the bargain of this newest generation is the SL-P110, which is barely half the size and weight of Technics' original SL-P10, and merely one quarter the price. Yet only the original unit's direct track-access feature and remote-control unit are missing from the SL-P110.

Technics now uses digital filtering and a single-beam laser (called "Fine-Focus"), rather than its original analog filters and triple-beam laser. The company claims it obtains smoother sound reproduction with more accurate tracking from its new technology. However, unlike many other units, the SL-P110 does not use oversampling with its digital filtering. Also, this CD player's shallow depth may cause problems when stacking it with other full-depth components.

CONTROL PANEL LAYOUT

The SL-P110's front panel embodies the essence of simplicity with flexibility. A power switch on the far left sits next to the disc drawer. The panel's center features the all-inclusive fluorescent display above a row of touch plates, which are, from left to right, drawer open/close, repeat, time mode for the display, memory/recall for programming, combination scan/search in either direction, stop/clear, and play/pause. (A slash indicates a dual function.) The disc drawer also closes by tapping its front. A blank panel at the far right replaces features, such as a remote-control sensor, found on more expensive models. The SL-P110 lacks a headphone jack.

The display panel flashes the word "disc" during loading and unloading; it remains illuminated when the CD is loaded. The panel also displays the number of tracks on the disc, all the way up to 99. Smaller digits to the right indicate four different time modes: remaining disc time, elapsed time from the beginning of the disc, current track number and remaining time of that track, and the current track number and elapsed playing time of that track.

In addition, the display informs you of your programming selections and their order. Since this CD player lacks numeric buttons for direct track access, programming is achieved by shuttling back and forth between tracks using the skip/search buttons. The repeat feature permits the repetition of virtually any segment. You can even program stopping and starting points by time, an unusual feature on such an inexpensive CD player. However, the SL-P110 does not display or acknowledge index points on a CD. Symbols on the display indicate the selected function.

This unit's rear panel contains only the power cord input and one pair of stereo output jacks.

USE AND LISTENING TESTS

Technic's new "high-speed linear access system" is indeed fast. The laser skips from track 1 to track 10 in barely over one second; such instantaneous performance is also unexpected in such a low-priced CD player. All of the controls responded positively and functioned without problems. The skip/search keys provide audible, two-speed scanning when depressed while playing a CD. The laser pickup moves slowly for the first three seconds, and it then accelerates while the output drops to one quarter of its normal volume. If skip/search is engaged during the stop mode, the search is silent. Skipping tracks forward or backward requires a quick, light touch.

Arguments about the sonic advantages between analog and digital filtering tend to be purely academic now that most CD players employ the latter method. However, the SL-P110 demonstrates that the sound of different players employing digital filtering is not identical. Whereas well-recorded CDs sounded quite good on the SL-P110, some discs sounded a bit harsh. While much of the blame for this falls on the recording, some of it is accentuated by the player.

ERROR CORRECTION AND TRACKING

Although Technics boasts about its superior, single-beam ("Fine-Focus") laser system, the SL-P110 stuttered at the 900-micron interruption in the information layer on our standard defects disc. However, it breezed through the simulated 800-micron dust particle and fingerprint smudge. This CD player made the transition smoothly between tracks 18 and 19 (which lacks any space), and could be skipped to track 19 without a problem. Please note that our review sample arrived with the protective laser lock-down screw unlocked. Without this safety feature, the CD player may have been damaged during shipping.

The SL-P110 resisted shock admirably. Slapping the top and sides caused little, if any, mistracking. This is a pleasant surprise from a budget player.

SUMMARY

Considering all of the features offered by the Technics SL-P110, along with its fully acceptable sound quality, this less-expensive Technics CD player rates high in value. Dealers occasionally discount most Technics products, which should make this model even more attractive.

YAMAHA CD-300

Yamaha Electronics Corp., USA

MANUFACTURER'S SPECIFICATIONS:

Frequency Response: 5 Hz to 20 KHz, +0.5 dB, -1.0 dB.
Signal-to-Noise Ratio: 98 dB.
Dynamic Range: 95 dB.
Total Harmonic Distortion: 0.004% (at 1 KHz).
Channel Separation: Better than 90 dB (at 1 KHz).
Number of Programmable Events: 9.
Audio Output Level: 2 volts at full output.
Dimensions: 13⅜ Wide x 3⅝ High x 11⅜ inches Deep.
Approximate Retail Price: $299.
Approximate Low Price: $269.

Yamaha refrains from manufacturing cheap stereo equipment, while almost all of its dealers offer only minimal discounts on Yamaha components. Thus,

Yamaha has earned a reputation as a prestigious manufacturer of stereo components, and it is understandable that the introduction of the budget-priced CD-300 raised some eyebrows. However, it also increased their sales figures, since the CD-300 has become one of the hottest-selling CD players on the market.

Yamaha waited out the initial surge of competing products, so the CD-300 is their third-generation CD player. It incorporates Yamaha's proprietary circuits that employ very large scale integration (VLSI), which puts over 10,000 electronic components on a single computer chip, permitting the inclusion of a wide array of features in a compact, inexpensive CD player. In fact, the CD-300's small width may restrict the stacking of other components on top of it. Yamaha has used digital filtering in all of their CD players, and the CD-300 is no exception.

CONTROL PANEL LAYOUT

The front panel has the disc drawer occupying its left half, with the power switch in the left corner below the drawer. A four-character, alphanumeric, red LED (light-emitting diode) display to the right of the drawer performs multiple functions; other labeled LEDs are also present. When you press the power button, the display shows a row of 4 dashes, and then, by displaying "dISC," prompts you to insert a CD. To the right of this display, beneath the caption "Optimum Control Music Access System," are indicators for repeat play, index search, and stop.

The actual controls are situated beneath the display. Three large, rectangular touch plates initiate drawer open/close, play, and pause/stop. To the right of these are four small, rectangular buttons. The first two, labeled "+" and "-" (rather than the customary arrows) are for skipping backward and forward between entire tracks, and the final two buttons are labeled with double arrows, and are used for scanning backward and forward.

Three similar buttons on the far right of the front panel are, from top to bottom, display, repeat, and program. The display key toggles the display between the track number, the elapsed time, and the total time on the disc; the latter can only be displayed when the player is in the stop mode, which is indicated by two lowercase "o" symbols. The display also indicates PLAY, End, and "P" (for program). Needless to say, only one function is shown at a time. A headphone jack, which lacks a volume-level control, occupies the lower right corner.

The rear panel contains only the power cord input and one pair of stereo output jacks.

USE AND LISTENING TESTS

The player's reasonably fast track-access time requires four seconds to skip from track 1 to track 10. However, the multifunctional display and lack of numeric direct-access keys necessitate a somewhat cumbersome programming procedure. A total of nine selections may be programmed.

Impressive sound quality emanates from this inexpensive, but not cheap, CD player. The smooth, even sound quality resembled that obtained from good CD players that cost twice as much as the CD-300.

ERROR CORRECTION AND TRACKING

The Yamaha CD-300 handled all the "roadblocks" presented by our defects test disc. Its three-beam laser and error-correction circuitry paid little heed to the 900-micron defect, although a faint click that is evident of error correction could occasionally be heard. The laser also successfully navigated the occasionally difficult transition between tracks 18 and 19, although it did miss the very beginning of track 19 when cued to that point.

This unit's Achilles' heel is its lack of shock resistance. Light tapping on top of the CD-300 results in obvious mistracking, while tapping the sides results in microphonics, which means you can actually hear the sound of your tapping amplified through your loudspeakers. In order to fully enjoy this otherwise fine Yamaha player, it should be in a shock- and vibration-free environment.

SUMMARY

Yamaha's CD-300 demonstrates just how far CD technology has advanced. This low-cost CD player lacks only conveniences, such as remote control, rather than useful features, while its exemplary fidelity suffers only from a lack of shock resistance. If size is a problem, the CD-300 fits into tight spaces, since it is somewhat smaller than most other components. Yamaha's price structure fosters few discounts, but even at its suggested list price, this CD player is a good value.

Prices may vary; call local stores and check current ads.

TOSHIBA XR-P9/XR-J9

Toshiba America, Inc.

MANUFACTURER'S SPECIFICATIONS:

Frequency Response: 5 Hz to 20 KHz, +0.5 dB, -1.5 dB.
Signal-to-Noise Ratio: N/A.
Dynamic Range: Over 84 dB.
Total Harmonic Distortion: 0.01% (at 1 KHz).
Channel Separation: Over 75 dB (at 1 KHz).
Number of Programmable Events: 16 (AC only).
Audio Output Level: Fixed, 1 volt.
Dimensions (XR-P9): 4 $\frac{31}{32}$ Wide x 1 $\frac{9}{16}$ High x 7 $\frac{1}{32}$ inches Deep.
Dimensions (XR-J9): 9 $\frac{27}{32}$ Wide x 1 $\frac{27}{32}$ High x 5 $\frac{1}{8}$ inches Deep.
Weight (XR-P9): 1.1 lbs. without battery.
Weight (XR-J9): 2.9 lbs.
Approximate Retail Price (XR-P9): $300.
Approximate Retail Price (XR-J9): $200.
Approximate Low Price (XR-P9): $259.
Approximate Low Price (XR-J9): $160.

Toshiba lacks the brand name recognition and glamour of some of the other Japanese manufacturers. It made a brief foray into a full line of stereo components before retreating into "packaged" music systems, personal portables, and video and CD players. Actually, Toshiba owns a controlling interest in a moderately high-end Japanese component manufacturer, so that its superior technology isn't wasted. While not on the tip of American tongues, the Toshiba name commands high regard in its homeland.

The XR-P9 and XR-J9 rate as three, not two, of the most unusual CD players in this buying guide. These two models can actually be counted as a trio of players. The XR-P9 portable CD player comes packaged with the accessories, including remote control, required to make it a bona fide home CD player. The XR-J9 is the exact same unit, except that it has a permanently built-in AC power supply and more conventional, rectangular component styling, thus making it permanently homebound. However, the XR-J9 lacks remote control.

The XR-P9 performs different tricks depending on whether it hangs from your shoulder or sits on a shelf. When used as a portable, it snaps onto a bulky external battery pack that holds six "C" cells. As far as we know, it is the only portable CD player that is supplied without a compact, rechargeable battery pack. As a portable, it performs all basic functions, such as skip and scan, while displaying track numbers and times on a liquid crystal display (LCD).

Detach the battery pack and slide on the wedge-shaped AC power adapter, and this tiny CD player becomes a stylish shelf unit that faces you at just the right angle. Snap in the remote-control receiver, and not only do you have wireless remote-control capabilities, but you also have 16-selection programming via the remote-control unit's direct-access numeric keypad.

The XR-J9 offers programming without the aid, or option, of the remote-control module and its numeric keypad. Both the XR-P9 and XR-J9 employ a three-beam laser and analog filtering.

CONTROL PANEL LAYOUT

Both CD players contain essentially the same front-panel controls, although in slightly different configurations. Toward the front left of the XR-P9 is a button that pops open the disc-loading door. (Both of these CD players are top-loading machines; they do not use a disc drawer.) A safety interlock prevents this button from being pushed accidentally. Adjacent and to the right is a recessed button with the triple function of pause/stop/memory, followed by two smaller buttons for skip/scan down and up (backward and forward), and a large play/repeat button.

Above these controls are a red power-on LED, the multifunctional LCD display, and a button that toggles the display through its various modes. The display not only indicates tracks, elapsed and remaining time, and programming memory, but it also shows the function that is engaged. On the sides of the XR-P9 are a power switch, volume control, miniature stereo headphone jack, and miniature stereo line-out jack; an adapter is required for the miniature line-out jack in order to utilize standard Hi-Fi patch cords.

The XR-J9's controls don't differ enough to warrant a complete description. However, its power switch (with its LED), standard quarter-inch headphone jack, and volume control are on the front edge, with conventional stereo output jacks on the rear.

USE AND LISTENING TESTS

The convenient size of both the XR-P9 and the slightly larger XR-J9 lets you install either unit where no CD player has gone before. In addition, the remote control included with the XR-P9 rates as one of those "gee whiz" features. It seems uncanny to be able to control (and program) such a tiny CD player from across the room.

When it gets too stuffy inside, you can simply unplug a few connections and take the XR-P9 to the beach. A major improvement to this CD player's portability would be an optional, slim, rechargeable battery pack, such as those provided by Technics and Sony with their portable CD players. Toshiba states that it is designing such a battery pack. Both of these Toshiba CD players respond well to commands, offering reasonably fast access times.

The sound quality of these Toshiba units mildly emphasizes the unpleasant nature of poorly recorded discs. They tend to produce just a hint of harshness when played through a good stereo system. However, when using headphones, the XR-P9 sounds just fine. On well-recorded discs, both CD players exhibit little, if any, unpleasantness; they fully reproduce the impressive sound inherent in CDs.

ERROR CORRECTION AND TRACKING

The Toshiba XR-P9 performed well with our defects test disc, matching the performance of other portable CD players, as well as budget-priced home units. It gracefully tracked the pitfalls of the defects disc, with only occasional hints of error-correction clicks. Since it was designed as a portable, the XR-P9 tracked in every position, including upside down. It even survived active bicycling with only the most minor mistracking. However, jogging taxes this CD player beyond forgiveness. Nevertheless, the XR-P9 shrugs off tapping that annoys many shelf models. The XR-J9 performed just as well, since it is virtually identical to the XR-P9.

SUMMARY

Toshiba's inspiration to break from the accepted Sony portable design with a unique dual-purpose CD player, the XR-P9, deserves accolades. This unit, weighing under two pounds with batteries, will satisfy plenty of people in a lot of places. If you don't need portability or remote control, and you have only a small space for your home unit and very little money to spend, you should consider the XR-J9.

MAGNAVOX FD1041BK

N.A.P. Consumer Electronics Corp.

MANUFACTURER'S SPECIFICATIONS:

Frequency Response: 20 Hz to 20 KHz, ±0.3 dB.
Signal-to-Noise Ratio: More than 90 dB.
Dynamic Range: More than 90 dB.
Total Harmonic Distortion: Less than 0.004% (at 1 KHz).
Channel Separation: More than 90 dB (at 1 KHz).
Number of Programmable Events: 20.
Audio Output Level: 2 volts at full output.
Dimensions: 12½ Wide x 3½ High x 11¾ inches Deep.
Approximate Retail Price: $240.
Approximate Low Price: $195.

Philips, the parent company of Magnavox, never received its fair share of the glory as one of the two codevelopers of the Compact Disc system. Philips even named the system "Compact Disc." During the CD's first year on the market, the general consensus held that the Philips-designed CD players, which used digital filtering, sounded better than most of the Japanese units employing analog filtering. That controversy is nearly academic now, since most Japanese companies also advocate digital filtering, although it is not executed in the exact same manner as in the Philips system.

The Belgian manufactured FD1041BK stands out as one of the very few CD players discussed here that is not made in Japan. It's also one of the few that's assembled on a plastic (polystyrene) chassis. The small size of the Magnavox FD1041BK, similar to the Yamaha CD-300, may cause some problem when stacking with standard-sized components. Conversely, it fits conveniently fits into tight spaces.

Philips retained most of its original CD player design, but it joined the crowd by using a disc drawer mechanism, instead of a slot. The company still uses a unique system employing 14-bit, rather than 16-bit, digital-to-analog conversion, which is compensated for by quadruple oversampling. Note that N.A.P Consumer Electronics Corporation, a North American Philips company, also markets their products under the Sylvania and Philco brand names, so you may find similar CD players being sold under these names.

CONTROL PANEL LAYOUT

A large square on/off button occupies the upper left of the FD1041BK's front panel. Next to this is the disc-loading drawer. A pair of two-inch-long function keys labeled on a hard-to-read thin strip comprise the top row of controls. The first of these two keys controls four functions: open, close, stop, and clear memory; it is labeled o/c stop/cm.

To the right of this is the second function key, which is for start/replay control. Beneath the o/c stop/cm key are the reverse and forward search keys. The pause function rates a two-inch key all to itself, which sits to the right of the search key. Beneath this are four small pushbuttons labeled "previous," "next," "progr/review," and "time/track."

At the upper right hand corner lies the four-digit, green LED display. This normally displays the track and index number, but it can be toggled with the time/track key to show the elapsed time while playing, or total disc time when initially loading the CD. It uniquely counts down the pauses between the tracks, displaying a "P" for pause.

This is one of the few CD players we tested that does not close the disc drawer when you tap on the drawer's front. The Magnavox FD1041BK is also one of the few units without a repeat key. In addition, it lacks a head-phone jack.

The rear panel contains the power cord and stereo output jacks. There is also a jack for connecting an optional remote-control module.

USE AND LISTENING TESTS

Philips CD players traditionally boast great sound and somewhat tentative mechanical performance; the FD1041BK is no exception. Skipping from track 1 to track 10 took about 5 seconds, which is rather long by contemporary standards. Strangely, the CD player waits a couple of seconds after you touch the skip button before it moves the pickup. All mechanical commands cause the CD player to produce a whirring noise, which disappears during playing.

This unit's sound quality rates among the best we have heard in our tests. Even some less-than-perfect

CDs delivered acceptable sound when played on this player, while well-recorded discs sounded excellent.

The FD1041BK lets you program by track and index number, but not by time. Since this CD player lacks a numeric keypad for direct track-access, you must press three keys, two of which are multifunctional, within 5 seconds of each other to store a program. The player accepts up to 20 tracks for programming.

ERROR CORRECTION AND TRACKING

Considering that Philips created the defects test disc that we use, it's not surprising that the Magnavox FD1041BK breezed through all of the simulated defects as if they were not there. However, during the rapid track-access test, it often started playing a second or two after the beginning of the track.

This player takes a beating before mistracking; whacking the top showed no apparent effect. We had to hit the sides hard enough to move the CD player before it mistracked.

SUMMARY

Philips requires that its electronic products be sold through department stores and mass merchandisers. In addition, its pricing policy promises that you will occasionally see some substantial discounts on this CD player. This Philips marketing strategy deprives its excellent CD players from some of the recognition they deserve. Some people assume that a CD player found in a discount chain store lacks the flamboyance or quality of one found in an audio specialty store. While the Magnavox FD1041BK seems mechanically flimsy, if you see it at an attractive price, and you like this unit, by all means, buy it.

CHAPTER 6

Car CD Player Reviews

When the Compact Disc was introduced in 1983, one of the CD format's codevelopers, the Philips Company of the Netherlands, predicted that it wouldn't be long before we would all be enjoying Compact Discs in our cars. At the time, the idea seemed incredible.

How could a low-powered laser beam ever track the microscopic digital "pits" inscribed beneath the clear surface of a CD in a moving car? Surely, the precise tracking requirements of a CD could never be maintained while traveling along in a moving vehicle, even on smooth roads, let alone on the innumerable streets filled with potholes, or chuckholes.

Barely one year after the first home CD players were introduced, Sony unveiled the first car CD unit. Small enough to be installed in the dashboard of almost any automobile, this first car CD player came in two forms: as an add-on CD player for those who already had car stereo systems, and as a complete, combination CD player/AM-FM receiver for people who were willing to forsake cassettes and substitute this combination unit for whatever had been previously mounted in their dashboards.

Not only did these first car CD players perform as well as typical home units, they also maintained their tracking capability on all but the roughest roads. During our tests, the first time a car CD player mistracked because of an unusually large bump or pothole, the only evidence of the mistracking was a very brief interruption, or muting, of the music; the CD then resumed playing almost immediately.

The mechanical shock mounting of those first car CD players was an engineering feat of no small proportions, and yet, amazingly, a second generation of car CD units has since emerged from several manufacturers. Some of these car CD players possess even better tracking capability than did those first units. In addition, Sony's CDX-A10 is also the very first multiple-disc player (a CD changer, if you prefer) that can be installed in an automobile.

After surveying the field of car CD players, we suggest that unless you are skilled at installing car stereos, you should obtain professional installation of your car Compact Disc player. Aside from that, you need not handle that car CD player any differently than the one in your home Hi-Fi system.

However, we do not recommend storing the Compact Discs themselves inside an automobile, especially during the cold winter months or hot summer days. Summer temperatures inside a car have been known to reach in excess of 150 degrees Fahrenheit; such heat is likely to permanently damage the CDs. While CD players like the Sony CDX-A10 are designed to operate under such extreme temperatures, you must remove the disc magazines (holders) from the vehicle when you leave the car for more than a minute or two.

While Sony is not the only manufacturer of car CD players, we think they make the two best units. In addition, even though we consider the CDX-A10 to be a "Best Buy," the CDX-R7 is also a very good value. Read the following reviews and then go to the store to test some car CD players for yourself; we're certain you will agree with our conclusions.

SONY CDX-A10

Sony Corp. of America

MANUFACTURER'S SPECIFICATIONS:

Frequency Response: 5 Hz to 20 KHz, ±1.0 dB.
Signal-to-Noise Ratio: More than 85 dB.
Dynamic Range: More than 90 dB.
Total Harmonic Distortion: Less than 0.015% at 1 KHz.
Channel Separation: More than 78 dB.
Number of Programmable Events: 10.
Number of Discs Handled: 10.
Audio Output Level: 1,200 millivolts.
Dimensions (Trunk Unit): 12¾ Wide x 5¼ High x 8¾
  inches Deep.
Approximate Retail Price: $1,000.
Approximate Low Price: $914.

Sony's model CDX-A10, also known as the "DiscJockey," is billed as the world's first CD changer specifically designed for use in a car. This ten-disc unit is offered either as a changer only, or with a fully integrated AM/FM synthesized tuner.

Whichever unit you buy, all that's needed up front for driver access is a tiny control unit that Sony calls the "DiscJockey Remote Commander." This thin, DIN-sized unit (a standard size for most current cars) can be mounted on your dashboard, or it can be installed on an optional control pad when adding the CDX-A10 to an existing tuner/cassette car unit. You may not wish to mount the commander so passengers can operate the unit with greater ease. Then you can store the commander under the front seat when it's not in use, for greater security.

The heart of the CDX-A10 is its special ten-disc changer, which is installed in your vehicle's trunk. The mechanism is built around a free-floating subsuspension intended to resist shock and road vibrations. The outer casing of the changer is built of dust-resistant, high-impact material. A logic control system allows for rapid access to any disc selection. The system can also send up to six different messages regarding its operational status directly to the Remote Commander's displays.

Pushing "play" on the commander "initializes" the ten-disc magazine (cartridge, or holder) that is held in the changer, and playback commences from the first disc regardless of its location in the magazine. Ten discs can provide more than ten hours of continuous music without changing the magazine in the CD changer.

You can buy extra Sony magazines at a suggested retail price of $19.95 each. Like those used with Pioneer's PD-M6 and Mitsubishi's DP-409R home CD changers, Sony's magazines can be used to store your

Car CD Player Reviews

CDs at home in groups based on musical style, type, or any other classification. (The Mitsubishi and Pioneer home CD changers are reviewed in Chapter 8.)

These magazines generally take up less space than the equivalent number of CD "jewel box" cases. You will be glad to know that the ten-disc cartridge used in the CDX-A10 works in Sony's brand new home CD changer. If you bought both of these CD players, you could easily transfer a magazine full of discs from your car to your home and back again.

If you're wondering what to do with the booklets that normally accompany each CD, Sony supplies a little transparent folder (similar to plastic credit-card holders) with ten "pockets" that are just the right size for the CD booklets.

A random music feature allows you to repeat or randomly select up to five selections from any of the ten discs. In addition, a "Program Play" feature lets you program ten selections from any of the ten discs, with memory maintained even if you change listening sources (such as switching to the tuner) during operation of the unit. Other playback options include direct selection by disc and track number, skipping from one selection to another in either direction, and scanning the music at ten times normal speed in either the forward or reverse direction.

The tuner module, available as an option, has no controls whatever. Its cable simply plugs into a receptacle on the back of the changer module; then, the Remote Commander serves a dual purpose. When you switch to the tuner, all of the commander's button functions change to those needed for tuning and operating the AM/FM tuner. The tuner mode offers 20 presets (ten FM and ten AM stations), automatic scan tuning, manual tuning, FM stereo/mono switching, and impulse noise-suppression circuitry.

The Sony CDX-A10 DiscJockey can also serve as a preamplifier for your current car audio system, offering bass and treble tone controls, as well as volume, balance, and fader controls.

In 1983, when we learned about the intricacies of manufacturing CD players during a visit to Philips in Europe, one of their engineers suggested that when car CD players appeared, they should include compressor circuits, since most driving conditions would limit the enjoyment of the full dynamic range recorded on CDs. That is, when the volume is adjusted so the musical crescendos aren't too loud, the soft parts of the music would be hidden, or buried, under road and car noises. If the very wide dynamic range of music reproduced from CDs could be compressed, at least temporarily during playback in a car, you could increase the volume to hear quiet passages without having the loud crescendos hurt your ears.

Early car CD players lacked such circuits, but now Sony practices what the Philips engineer first preached. The CDX-A10 comes equipped with a dynamic range compressor, or "Suppressor," as they call it. Sony has also included a "Surround-Sound" circuit should you want to feed a bit of Surround-Sound ambience to the rear speakers while regular stereo program material emanates from the front speakers; this feature can be turned off, if you wish.

CONTROL LAYOUT OF THE REMOTE COMMANDER

To keep the commander module as small as it is (just over 7 inches wide by 2 inches high by 1 inch thick), Sony cleverly assigned multiple functions to the front-panel controls. The "Up/Down" volume-control button, for example, also alters tone-control settings, channel balance, and even front/rear fader settings; its function is determined by a small associated "Select" key. Pressing the "Select" key successively lights indicators that display the functions of the "Up/Down" buttons. The usual keys normally found on any CD player's control panel also appear on this tiny commander module, as are numbered keys for programming desired selections.

A key at the panel's lower right switches you over to the tuner, if you have connected the optional AM/FM tuner pack, and then, as if by magic, all of the previous CD displays and buttons that operated that player suddenly become AM/FM tuner controls. Keys previously used for fast music search and CD track advance now became manual and automatic radio tuning keys. Numbered buttons now call upon preset AM and FM stations. In addition, the large display window now tells you the frequency to which you are tuned, whether reception is mono or stereo, what preset number you have selected, and whether you are in the "local" or "distant" reception mode.

Mind you, all that's connecting this tiny commander module to the main unit in the trunk is a thin multiconductor cable that's easily hidden beneath the carpeting of your car. A small hole through the rear wall of the car's interior is all that's needed to pass this cable into the trunk space.

OUR LAB MEASUREMENTS

Frequency response for the Sony CDX-A10 varied no more than one third of a decibel from 20 Hz to 20 KHz. The signal-to-noise ratio was better than Sony claims, matching many home CD players. Harmonic and intermodulation distortion were acceptably low. Separation of 73 dB was quite a bit less than what we have come to expect from home CD players, but it was more than adequate for a good stereo effect.

Dynamic range reached an incredibly high 114 dB, while access time from one track to the next was actually less than 1 second. When the Remote Commander was instructed to go from one disc stored in the ten-disc cartridge to a different disc, that operation took about 12 seconds.

ERROR CORRECTION AND TRACKING

As expected, this Sony car CD player handled our defects test disc as if it had no imperfections. The CDX-A10 played all the way through the scratch, dust particle, and fingerprint smudge simulations with ease; there was no evidence of mistracking.

SUMMARY

We found the Sony car CD changer both easy to use and easy to load. The nice thing about this cartridge arrangement is that you can load up to ten discs into the magazine, and then travel along the highway for 500 miles or more without ever having to listen to the same musical selection.

This unit's sound quality and ease of use were impressive on the test bench and in the listening room, as well as on the road. We suspect that the two compression settings will be appreciated by audio buffs who want to listen to CDs in a car without either rupturing the cones of their car speakers or turning the volume so low as to miss the quieter passages of music. We found the compression settings to be extremely effective; they were set ideally for both actual driving conditions and the road noises associated with city or highway driving.

Certainly, the price of this car CD changer is quite high, but the technology required to create this unique CD player is very sophisticated and well worth the price. In addition, when you consider the costs of other car CD players, the Sony CDX-A10, with all of its extra features, is an excellent value.

SONY CDX-R7

Sony Corp. of America

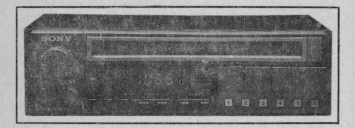

MANUFACTURER'S SPECIFICATIONS:

Frequency Response: 5 Hz to 20 KHz.
Signal-to-Noise Ratio: More than 90 dB.
Dynamic Range: More than 90 dB.
Total Harmonic Distortion: Less than 0.005%.
Channel Separation: 95 dB.
Number of Programmable Events: None.
Audio Output Level: 2.0 volts rms.
Dimensions: DIN-E standard 178 Wide x 50 High x 155 millimeters Deep (approximately 7 x 2 x 6 inches)
Approximate Retail Price: $700.
Approximate Low Price: $659.

Sony Corporation, codeveloper of the CD format, offers two single-disc car CD players. We tested their model CDX-R7, which includes a complete AM/FM stereo tuner and preamp-control section. Amazingly, this product fits into the DIN-E-sized opening found in European-made cars. (DIN is an acronym for Deutsche Industrie Normen, a German standard for the production of a wide variety of equipment; DIN-E is a new version of this standard.) Actually, Sony claims the CDX-R7 will fit into the dashboards in virtually all current European, domestic, and Japanese cars, although they wisely advise that you make sure it will fit before you buy any car CD player.

According to Sony, the two primary designs that were needed to make a practical car CD player were in the area of the laser optical pickup and in circuitry that employed very large scale integration (VLSI, a means of putting a great number of electronic components on a single computer chip). Since Sony has their own IC (integrated circuit) design and production division, they were able to develop a new, specific, digital VLSI chip to perform all primary functions of their proposed car Compact Disc player.

Sony also developed a miniaturized laser optic mechanism that facilitates not only the design of car CD players, but "Walkman"-type CD units as well. (See Chapter 7 for reviews of portable CD players; also read about Toshiba's XR-P9 home/portable CD player in Chapter 5.) This miniaturization was made possible, in part, by housing much of the tuner circuitry in a separate, flat container, which was devoid of controls, that could be mounted away from the main section of the unit. The two parts are connected by means of a multi-conductor cable and two stereo cables.

CONTROL PANEL LAYOUT

The front panel of the Sony CDX-R7 is no larger than that of any in-dash car stereo. Along the top edge of its front panel is a slot, or door, into which the CD is placed. When you insert a disc partway, the mechanism draws the CD into the machine, placing it in position for play. Push the "Eject" button at the slot's far right, and the disc comes out partially. If you don't remove it within 15 seconds, the CD is reloaded and held in the pause mode; this arrangement protects the disc from dust and damage. If you then fail to release the pause mode within 15 minutes, the CD player's power turns off completely.

The front panel's left end houses the usual concentric volume, fader, and balance controls, as well as separate bass and treble tone knobs. A switch beneath the disc slot's left end determines what will be visible in the nearby display area. When playing a CD, touching this switch alters the display from the time of day (clock function) to the track number of the disc being played. Unlike home CD players, this unit does not tell you the elapsed time in a given track. When using the built-in AM-FM tuner, the same display alternates between the time of day and the frequency of the station you've selected.

A local/distant switch and a stereo/mono switch along the panel's lower edge govern only FM reception. Other controls that affect only the tuner include an AM/FM band selector switch, a tuner on/off switch, and six numbered preset buttons. Secondary buttons labeled "FM1," "FM2," and "AM" work in conjunction with the presets, so you can have the CDX-R7 "memorize" up to 18 stations (12 FM and 6 AM). A "Play/Pause" button at the far right of the front panel performs the same function during CD play as that control does on home CD players.

The remaining controls and switches beneath the display area, however, serve different purposes depending on whether you are listening to a disc or to the tuner. A memory button is used to memorize preset station frequencies in the tuner mode, but when you are listening to CDs, this same button returns the laser pickup to the beginning of a disc in order to replay the first track.

Other dual-purpose switches under the display area include the fast forward/rewind switch used to scan quickly through the music on a disc (at 10 times normal speed and a much lower volume); it serves as a manual-tuning rocker switch in the tuner mode. A second rocker switch lets you advance to the next (or previous) track of a CD, just as in Sony's home CD players. However, this second rocker switch becomes a scanning control in the tuner mode, pausing for four seconds at each station, so you can decide whether to listen to that station or continue scanning.

A single integrated circuit (IC), or computer chip, developed for digital signal processing of CD signals, combines the nine separate functions previously performed by as many as five separate ICs. This chip may be safely stored at any temperature from -55 to +150 degrees Celsius (about -67 to +302 degrees Fahrenheit, respectively), and it can be operated at temperatures ranging from -20 to +75 degrees Celsius (about -4 to +167 degrees Fahrenheit). This ability to work over such a wide temperature range is essential for any device intended for use in the hostile and extreme environment inside an automobile.

A new laser pickup assembly developed for this car CD player occupies about one third of the space and weighs about one third as much as the previous pickup assembly used in Sony home CD players. This miniaturization does not sacrifice any of the elements needed for accurate and stable servo-tracking and focusing of the laser beam onto the precise area (and depth) of the CD for accurate reading of the digital information embedded below its surface.

OUR LAB MEASUREMENTS

We measured the performance of the CDX-R7 both as an AM/FM stereo tuner and as a full-function car CD player. Our test showed that this was one of the most sensitive tuners we have tested. Frequency response of the CD player section varied no more than one third of a decibel over the entire audio range (20 Hz to 20 KHz). Harmonic distortion and intermodulation (IM) distortion were negligible. The signal-to-noise ratio was nearly 92 dB, a bit less than most home CD players. Separation between left- and right-channel signals was more than 80 dB. Output linearity was accurate to within 0.2 dB from the maximum recording level down to 80.0 dB below that level.

Harmonic distortion in mono measured 0.15%, while in the stereo reception mode, it increased very slightly to 0.18%. Signal-to-noise ratio for strong FM signals was 72 dB for mono and 70 dB for stereo. Stereo separation measured nearly 40 dB at mid-frequencies, and almost as high (38 dB) at higher frequency extremes. Tuner output level was just over 1.0 volt, enough to drive most car stereo power amplifiers (you must use a power amp with the CDX-R7). Frequency response was virtually flat from 30 Hz to 10 KHz, and exhibited a slight dip of around -2.5 dB at 15 KHz, the top FM transmitted audio frequency.

ERROR CORRECTION AND TRACKING

Once again we used our special test disc that contains simulated defects, such as scratches (of varying widths) and dust particles (of varying diameters), superimposed on identified musical selections. Only the better home CD players are able to get through this obstacle course with no evidence of mistracking. The Sony CDX-R7 did so without difficulty, "overlooking" missing digital code that was at least 900 microns in length.

We also subjected the CDX-R7 to a fair amount of vibration and shock, induced by thumping on its top and sides. In spite of this, the pickup continued to track those microscopic pits beneath the surface of the Compact Disc without ever mistracking.

SUMMARY

We took the CDX-R7 and a few of our favorite CDs for a test drive. Along well-paved highways there was not the slightest glitch or mistracking. Only when we ran through some really severe potholes or over major bumps did the CDX-R7 start to mute, momentarily, as it mistracked. Once past the defect in the road, the music returned almost immediately, and nine times out of ten, the pickup continued playing from the point of interruption. On one occasion, it had moved enough to begin playing another track.

Bear in mind that we were deliberately trying to get the unit to mistrack. Under average driving conditions, you can expect no more problems than you experience with an ordinary car cassette player—which means virtually no mistracking whatsoever.

Whether or not you own a home CD player, you can now enjoy listening to CDs on the road. The quality and performance of the Sony CDX-R7 seems to justify the cost. Just remember that you need a separate power amplifier to use this unit; you may also want to evaluate your current car speaker system.

CHAPTER 7

Portable CD Player Reviews

If you think car CD players are a technological miracle, just imagine what problems had to be solved to create a CD player that could be carried around wherever you go, much as listeners do with those ubiquitous "Walkman"-type, personal portable cassette players. Yet, the seemingly impossible task of miniaturizing a full-featured CD player and getting it to operate for a reasonable length of time on limited battery power has been achieved. Furthermore, there are now several companies offering such portables; the most notable are Sony and Technics.

About two years ago, Sony introduced the first portable CD player; by today's standards, it was a "bare-bones" model. Not to be outdone, Technics (the High-Fidelity component division of Matsushita Electric Corporation of America, which also markets its products under the Panasonic and Quasar brand names) unveiled a feature-laden portable CD player just a few months later. Technics' model SL-XP7 allowed for, among other things, random-access programming of 15 selections on a disc, much as you can do with home CD players.

Never one to avoid a battle for technological supremacy, Sony created their "second-generation" portable CD player, the D-7 "Discman." Boasting marginally smaller dimensions (only a fraction of an inch) than the Technics SL-XP7, the Sony D-7 also claimed somewhat longer operation for each recharge of its battery. However, Technics recently announced a new portable CD player, the SL-XP5, which replaces the SL-XP7. In an effort to gain the lead over Sony, Technics reduced the unit's height (by only 0.36 inches) and upgraded a few features.

Other portable CD players are now offered by other companies, including Pioneer. However, we feel that the Technics and Sony models are outstanding in their class, with the Sony D-7 edging out the Technics SL-XP5 for "Best Buy" honors. Another unit worth considering is the Toshiba XR-P9, which can serve as either a portable player or a home unit; we reviewed it in Chapter 5.

SONY D-7

Sony Corp. of America

MANUFACTURER'S SPECIFICATIONS:

Frequency Response: 20 Hz to 20 KHz, +1 dB, -3 dB.
Signal-to-Noise Ratio: 90 dB.

Dynamic Range: More than 90 dB.
Total Harmonic Distortion: Less than 0.008%.
Channel Separation: More than 85 dB.
Number of Programmable Events: 16.
Audio Output Level: 1.6 volts rms.
Dimensions: 4⅞ Wide x ¹⁵⁄₁₆ High x 5 inches Deep.
Weight: 1.12 lbs.; 2.2 lbs. including rechargeable battery.
Approximate Retail Price: $300.
Approximate Low Price: $269.

The first company to market a portable CD player has taken another leap ahead. Perhaps Sony's new D-7 "Discman" was inspired by the Technics SL-XP7 portable unit that outclassed the older Sony D-5 in features and programmability. However, considering how long it takes to develop a product like the D-7, Sony probably had planned to outdo its original D-5 all along.

In any case, the D-7 CD player is an amazing engineering achievement. Not only is it one of the two smallest CD portables in the world (Technics SL-XP5 is the other), but its new carrying case adds very little to its width and depth, since its rechargeable battery pack sits below the CD player, rather than behind it, as in the earlier D-5.

With the earlier D-5, you had to pay an extra $50 or so for the battery pack/carrying case. These items are now included with the D-7, as is an AC adapter. (Technics also decided to supply the battery pack and carrying case with their newer SL-XP5 portable; again, these items were options for the older Technics SL-XP7.) The new battery pack lets you operate the player for around 4½ hours, as compared to the battery pack that's included with the Technics SL-XP5, which lasts for up to five hours.

Even if your needs extend beyond the operating time of the rechargeable battery, you can buy a battery case, which accepts eight alkaline "AA" cells and gives you three more hours of playing time. The "AA" batteries are replaceable, but not rechargeable. However, if you want to listen to CDs away from home for more than 4½ hours, the cost of eight "AA" batteries is a reasonable price to pay.

Like the older D-5, the D-7 provides quick track selection, two-speed audible music search, and Play/Pause/Stop controls. In addition, the new unit lets you program as many as 16 CD tracks to be played in any order. You can also repeat an entire disc, a single track, or a short phrase of music that you specify. A special feature that Sony introduced on some of their more expensive home CD players is called "Shuffle Play." This function makes the D-7 play all the songs on a CD in a random order, over and over again. You never hear the songs in the same order as long as Shuffle Play is operating.

CONTROL PANEL LAYOUT

When we first read about all of the control features on the D-7, we wondered how so many functions could be activated using so few front-panel controls. We discovered that Sony cleverly designed many of the tiny buttons to perform two or three functions.

For instance, the "Play/Pause" key initiates CD play when pressed the first time. Pressed a second time, it engages the "Pause" mode. Play is resumed by pressing this key again. The "Stop" key not only ends play, but it also turns off the power to conserve battery life. The forward and reverse "Search" keys operate in two ways, depending on whether you are in the "music search" mode or "track advance" mode. In the first case, pressing these search keys allows audible fast-cueing to a desired point. Alternatively, these keys can be used to reach the beginning of a desired track. A "Key Mode" key lets you select whichever of these modes you want.

A "Play Mode" key successively selects five different playing functions: normal play, all repeat play, A-to-B repeat play, "shuffle" repeat play, or, if the player has been programmed randomly, play of desired selections in a specific order. A remain/enter key also serves multiple functions, besides varying the time and track display on the liquid crystal display (LCD) area nearby. During the A-to-B repeat play mode, this key is used to enter the starting ("A") and ending ("B") points of the musical phrase you want repeated. When in the programming mode, this same key is used to "memorize" each track number as it is programmed.

All of these various modes of operation are visually confirmed on the adjacent liquid crystal display. The LCD also shows battery condition, elapsed and remaining playback times, and the tracks remaining or the track that's currently playing.

A miniature headphone output jack, headphone volume control, and main power on/off switch are located along the right side panel of the D-7. The power switch insures that play won't accidentally begin during transport of the player if one of the operation keys is depressed, even though pushing the "Stop" button also turns off the power. The rear panel of the D-7 houses the miniature stereo "Line Out" jack and a "DC IN" jack to which the AC adapter or an optional car battery cord is connected when the unit is not powered by its battery pack.

The D-7 is a top-loading CD player. Depressing a button atop the player opens its lid for disc mounting. Whenever the lid is open, an automatic safety switch disengages the D-7's motor and turns off the laser beam. A transparent "window" in the top cover lets you see part of a mounted disc when the cover is in the closed position.

OUR LAB MEASUREMENTS

We measured this portable CD player using its own battery pack, rather than employing its AC adapter, since most users will operate the player in this manner. We did, however, repeat some measurements, such as signal-to-noise ratio, using the AC adapter, since we wanted to make certain that the use of the adapter did not degrade signal-to-noise performance because of power supply hum or other noise components. The S/N measurements turned out to be very similar regardless of the power source.

Frequency response of the D 7 varied little from 20 Hz to 10 KHz, with a slight dip beginning just above 10 KHz and reaching a substantial attenuation of 3.5 dB at the top test frequency of 20 KHz.

The signal-to-noise ratio rated about the same as for the average home CD player. Total harmonic distortion measured unusually low, and intermodulation distortion was better than acceptable. Linearity was nearly perfect from 0 dB down to -80 dB output levels, with deviation from perfect linearity never exceeding 0.2 dB over that entire range.

Stereo separation ranged from less than 60 dB at the high frequencies to 83.3 dB at the middle and low frequencies. Separation for this unit, as well as for other portable CD players we measured, was one of the few parameters that was not as good as in larger CD players. We doubt if it has anything to do with the digital circuit sections of the player. The decreased separation may be caused, in part, by inadequacies in the shielding of the supplied line-out audio cable itself. In any event, even 60 dB of separation between channels is really nothing worth complaining about in terms of audible stereo effects.

Short access time (the time it takes for the laser pickup to move from the track that is playing to the next track, using the track advance keys) was no more than 1 second. On the other hand, long access time (the time it takes to move from an inner track to an outer track, using the programming mode) was close to 6 seconds. Reproduction of a 1 KHz square wave by the D-7 was typical of that produced by CD players employing steep, analog multipole filters.

ERROR CORRECTION AND TRACKING

This CD player was much less susceptible to external shock and vibration than was the earlier D-5. The D-7 not only was able to play through our simulations of scratches, dust specks, and a fingerprint smudge, but its resistance to vibration and shocks applied to its top surface were incredible, to say the least.

SUMMARY

The Sony D-7 Discman is, in our opinion, the most cleverly designed portable CD player that we have seen thus far. The liquid crystal display offers enough information so that even without an owner's manual, a new user will have no difficulty figuring out and using this CD player's many features.

Effective styling, ultra miniaturization, and resistance to shock and vibration are all important attributes for a portable CD player. What counts even more, though, is the quality of sound reproduction. If we weren't aware that musical test discs were being played with a slight decrease of the high frequencies, we could have easily believed that the music reproduced by this portable unit was being played on a full-sized, expensive CD player. In a word, the D-7 sounds great. If the original D-5 suffered from any shortage of features, such as programmability, the D-7 takes care of those omissions and then some.

Frankly, if someone had told us two years ago that it would be possible to squeeze all of that circuitry, plus a turntable, motor, and laser pickup, into the small volume occupied by the Sony D-7, we would have questioned their sanity. Yet, even after our hands-on evaluation of this extraordinary unit, we still find it to be totally amazing.

TECHNICS SL-XP5

Technics

MANUFACTURER'S SPECIFICATIONS:

Frequency Response: 4 Hz to 20 KHz, +0.5, -1.0 dB.
Signal-to-Noise Ratio: 90 dB.
Dynamic Range: 90 dB.
Total Harmonic Distortion: 0.006%.
Channel Separation: 90 dB.
Number of Programmable Events: 18.
Audio Output Level: 1.8 volts.
Dimensions: 4.96 Wide x 0.9 High x 4.96 inches Deep.
Weight: 1.1 lbs.
Approximate Retail Price: $300.
Approximate Low Price: $269.

While neither company would readily admit it, it's no secret that Matsushita Electric (the parent company of Technics) and Sony are forever trying to outdo each other when it comes to innovations in consumer product technology. To Sony goes the credit for coming up with the world's first portable CD player. That unit, the D-5, was introduced nearly two years ago, and it was very well received.

Sony, however, was soon surpassed by Technics and their SL-XP7 portable CD player, which had the most features in the smallest package. Then Sony took the lead with their D-7 "Discman," and again, Technics changed the tide with their SL-XP5. Its width and depth (4.96 inches each) are barely larger than the diameter (4.72 inches) of a Compact Disc. Plus, the Technics SL-XP5 just beats the Sony D-7 in two (height and depth) out of the three dimensions.

The most important feature of the Technics SL-XP5 (and its predecessor, the SL-XP7) that was not offered on the older Sony D-5 is random-access programming. The SL-XP5 lets you program up to 18 selections on a disc to be played in any order you choose, as compared to the SL-XP7's 15 choices and the Sony D-7's 16 selections. In addition, the SL-XP5 offers the usual conveniences found on most home CD players, such as forward and backward skipping of tracks, forward and backward audible fast search, and repeat play.

The SL-XP5 has two miniature stereo output jacks, one for connection to a home stereo system, the other for a pair of headphones. Besides a volume control, the headphone jack also has a high-cut filter that affects only that jack's output. Some people find that when they listen to CDs through headphones, the treble seems a bit too shrill. Turning on the high-cut filter provides a gentle "roll-off" above 3 KHz or so, which eases the load on your ears.

An LCD (liquid crystal display) on the front of the unit provides as much information about the status of the SL-XP5 and the disc being played as do the displays found on larger, home CD players. The display indicates the total number of tracks and total playing time (both are displayed when a CD is first inserted and scanned), track number being played, elapsed or remaining time, the programmed order of tracks, a confirmation that the "Repeat" function has been activated, and a warning of low battery voltage.

The SL-XP5 now comes with a carrying case and rechargeable battery pack; these were options for the SL-XP7. (Sony also decided to include these two items when they upgraded the D-5 to the D-7.) The battery pack is exactly as wide and deep as the SL-XP5 itself, adding just 0.47 inches to the CD player's height. The SL-XP5 is also supplied with an AC adapter, while a car battery adapter is offered as an option. The SL-XP5's battery pack can play for up to five hours. However, unlike Sony's D-7, which can use replaceable alkaline cells, the SL-XP5's power must come from the "NiCad" batteries in its battery pack.

CONTROL PANEL LAYOUT

Press the button at the left, on the top of the SL-XP5, and the top cover opens, exposing a turntable onto which you place a disc. If the unit's power is switched on when you close the cover, the turntable starts spinning. Then the laser pickup scans the CD, and the total number of tracks and total playing time are shown on the front panel's display. Press the play/pause button on the right side of the top surface, and the CD starts to play from the beginning.

Located near the front-panel display area are buttons labeled "Memory/Recall" (for storing programmed tracks and reviewing your selected program sequences), "Remain Time" (which alters the display during play from elapsed track time to remaining time), and "Repeat." The repeat function will cause either a single track, all programmed tracks, or the entire disc to be played repeatedly, depending on what mode of play you selected initially. Three larger buttons, near the right edge of the front panel, are used for the forward/skip functions, to stop play, and to clear a previously memorized program.

The power "On/Off" switch is located along the left side panel of this CD player, while the "Line Out" miniature stereo jack and the DC input terminal are found on the rear panel. The right side panel houses the headphones output jack, its associated thumb-wheel volume control, and the on/off switch for the headphone jack's high-cut filter.

OUR LAB MEASUREMENTS

Since the SL-XP5 was announced just before this book went to the presses, we did not get a chance to measure it in our laboratory. However, since the

SL-XP5 includes some changes, such as a new lens in its laser pickup and an improved "Digital Accu-Servo System" (for better error correction), it is quite likely that the following results for the SL-XP7 will be improved upon by the SL-XP5.

Frequency response of the SL-XP7 was essentially flat from 20 Hz to 20 KHz, with a slight rise near the high end amounting to no more than about one third of a decibel, followed by a decline of about one half of a decibel at the very high end, although this was not equal in both channels. We also measured the response of the CD player with its high-cut filter turned on. Frequencies above 2 or 3 KHz are attenuated at a rate of 3 to 4 decibels per octave, resulting in a -10 dB roll-off at 20 KHz.

Total harmonic distortion measured unusually low, and intermodulation distortion was low as well. Linearity was nearly perfect from 0 dB down to -80 dB output levels, while the signal-to-noise ratio was slightly below that of the better home CD players. Stereo separation ranged from 60.2 dB at high frequencies to 88.4 dB at middle and low frequencies. Reproduction of a square wave by the SL-XP7 was typical of that produced by CD players employing steep, analog multipole filters. As is true of most CD players that use analog filters, the SL-XP7 showed substantial phase shift, or time delay, when reproducing high-frequency signals.

ERROR CORRECTION AND TRACKING

Since this CD player was designed for use as either a portable or a home unit, Technics paid special attention to providing good tracking and error correction. Not only was the SL-XP7 able to "ignore" our simulations of scratches, dust specks, and the fingerprint smudge, but its resistance to vibration and shocks to its top surface were incredible, to say the least.

The Technics SL-XP7 is not intended for use by joggers—at least not while they are jogging. We did, however, subject the unit to a very practical test that should give you some idea of the incredible stability of its tracking system.

Larry Schotz, a well known Wisconsin inventor who has designed circuits and products for such noted firms as NAD, Proton, Nakamichi, Crown International, and Recoton, has come up with what we think is an ideal way to use portable CD players in cars. The adapter he devised (which, incidentally, is now sold by Recoton as their Model CD-20) requires no physical wiring or connection to your existing car stereo system. Yet, when used properly, this adapter will deliver the full, flat frequency response from a CD and, if your car stereo amplifier can handle it, the full dynamic range of a CD as well.

This device resembles an audio cassette, but is, in reality, an adapter that connects to the headphone output of a portable CD player. The adapter also contains a tape head that, in essence, transfers the signals from your portable CD player into the cassette playback section of your car stereo system.

Testing the SL-XP7 with this adapter, we drove over several shopping mall "speed bumps" at somewhat more than the speed (five miles per hour) for which they were intended. With the Technics CD player simply resting on the seat of our test vehicle, it did not mistrack or skip even once. The same held true for more ordinary driving.

We suspect that portable CD players will prove to be the ideal solution for people who want CD-quality sound in their cars, but aren't ready to mount CD players in or under the dash for fear of theft or simply because of the high cost of car units. The nice thing about using a portable CD player in this manner is that when you are through driving, you can simply pick up the CD player in one hand and the tiny Recoton adapter in the other, and take them both home, where they will be safe for the night.

SUMMARY

The various convenience features of the Technics player all worked perfectly, including the programming and handy display functions. Sound quality, which should still be a primary concern for anyone thinking to invest in a CD player, was excellent. There were some CDs to which we listened using a good pair of headphones that benefited greatly when we turned on the high-cut filter. As with any signal modifier, it's always nice to be able to turn it off when you don't think it's required. Fortunately, that's exactly what you can do with the new Technics SL-XP5, which makes it an even better value.

CHAPTER 8

CD Changer Reviews

In High-Fidelity circles, the once popular record changer became shunned in favor of single-disc turntables, and for good reason. Anyone who values their LP record collection watches uncomfortably as one record crashes onto another, contemplating the possible damage that could result from such an operation. Also, as the record stack builds up on the turntable, the angle between the phonograph stylus (needle) and the record groove changes, resulting in less than optimum sound reproduction.

Both of these problems disappear when using a CD player. Nothing touches the disc as it spins inside the player. So, despite the fact that CDs can hold more recorded music than LPs (CDs can play for up to 74 minutes, their theoretical limit), several manufacturers reasoned that some consumers might like the idea of a multiple-CD player.

Technics announced the first CD changer, which stored and handled as many as 50 discs! While some of these units were sold in Japan, none of them ever reached the States, as far as we have been able to determine, although a revised model for U.S. distribution is in the offing.

The first multiple-disc player to be sold in the U.S. was the Pioneer PD-M6, a player that used a CD cartridge to hold six discs. This was followed by a Nikko unit that can handle up to 60 discs. However, because of its physical configuration, the Nikko CD changer is better suited for professional use (disco, radio station, and the like) than as a home unit.

We have already discussed Sony's CDX-A10 Car CD Changer in Chapter 6, and by the time you read this,

Sony will have released their own home CD changer, model CDP-C10, at a suggested retail price of $799.95. This home CD changer accommodates the same ten-disc cartridge used in that company's car CD changer, so that cartridges ($19.95 retail) loaded with discs can be transferred easily from home to car, without unloading and reloading the CD cartridge.

This Sony home CD player was not available in time for us to measure it in our laboratory. However, judging from the performance of other Sony CD players and their car CD changer, the CDP-C10 home CD changer should be considered if you like the idea of sitting back in your easy chair and listening to hours of uninterrupted music reproduced from ten discs.

Besides the aforementioned Pioneer PD-M6 CD changer, we also evaluated the Mitsubishi DP-409R CD changer. This Mitsubishi unit employs a CD cartridge that can hold as many as five CDs, as opposed to the Pioneer and Sony cartridges that can handle six and ten discs, respectively. Remember that even though we rated the Pioneer CD changer as a "Best Buy," the Mitsubishi unit is also a very good value.

PIONEER PD-M6

✓ **BEST BUY**

Pioneer Electronics (USA) Inc.

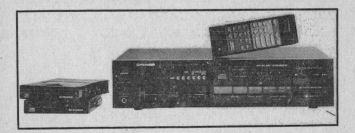

MANUFACTURER'S SPECIFICATIONS:

Frequency Response: 4 Hz to 20 KHz, -0.1 dB.
Signal-to-Noise Ratio: Greater than 98 dB.
Dynamic Range: Greater than 94 dB.
Total Harmonic Distortion: Less than 0.005%.
Channel Separation: Greater than 92 dB.
Number of Programmable Events: 32.
Number of Discs Handled: 6.
Audio Output Level: 2.0 volts rms.
Dimensions: 16 9/16 Wide x 3 7/8 High x 12 7/16 inches Deep.
Approximate Retail Price: $500.
Approximate Low Price: $444.

The PD-M6 can play any of six discs loaded in a magazine, or cartridge, with random-access programming of up to 32 tracks on any of the discs. Direct access to any track on any disc is also easily accomplished. Repeat functions are available for repeat play of all six discs, one track of one disc, or all programmed tracks on any of the six discs. Audible scan of program material is offered at two speeds.

The PD-M6 has a headphone output with an independent volume control. A wireless, hand-held remote control allows you to operate the CD player's functions at a distance, and it even permits full programming of the player. The Pioneer PD-M6 is also equipped with a subcode output connector for CD graphics adapters, when they become available.

CONTROL PANEL LAYOUT

Because the PD-M6 accepts the wide six-disc magazine in its loading slot, if you want to play a single disc, you must load that CD into a "single-disc magazine" (holder) that, along with the six-disc magazine, comes with the player. This loading slot, about as wide as the tape slot in a videocassette recorder, is situated below a multifunctional display area on the front panel. The "Power" on/off button and the headphone jack with its volume control are located to the left of the slot and display area.

The fluorescent display area indicates: "Repeat" play; "Program" memorization; program step or time in minutes; disc number (1 through 6) or time in seconds; track number; and, in diagrammatic form, which disc is being played. Numbered touch buttons to the right of the display let you select the disc number, while, just below, smaller, numbered (0 through 9) buttons let you choose tracks to be played or programmed. Larger, light-touch buttons below all of the numbered buttons are used for ejecting the disc magazine, repeat play, program memorization, and track advance or reverse search.

A small "Display" key below this bank of buttons changes a portion of the display from elapsed playback time to total playback time and the total number of tracks on the disc in use. If this key is pressed twice, the display shows the disc number and track number. If this key is pressed again, the display changes back to its original mode. A "Check" key to the right of the "Display" key lets you check the contents of a previously entered program, item by item, while a nearby "Clear" key allows you to erase previously entered program commands.

To the right of the "Check" and "Clear" keys lies a button labeled "Random Play," which is another innovation offered by this player. Push this button after you've loaded six discs into the player, and the PD-M6 will play tracks on all discs, in random order, continually until you stop the machine. "Play" and "Pause" buttons lie at the right end of the front panel, and below them are the two-speed forward and backward manual (audible) search buttons. If pressed for more than two seconds, these buttons increase the speed of the audible search. A "Stop" button is found at the lower right of the front panel.

OUR LAB MEASUREMENTS

Frequency response of the Pioneer PD-M6 decreased about three quarters of a decibel at the high-frequency end of the audio spectrum. The harmonic and intermodulation distortions produced by this well-designed CD player were almost negligible.

The signal-to-noise ratio was very good, much better than claimed by Pioneer. Stereo separation ranged from 71.0 dB at the high-frequency extremes to 88.0 dB at mid-frequencies. Dynamic range for this player measured 100 dB; that's considerably better than the 96 dB reported in the owner's manual. Reproduction of a 1 KHz square wave by the PD-M6 produced a waveform that is typically produced by CD players employing steep analog filters.

Two access-time measurements were made. The first, called "short access," times the laser pickup assembly as it moves from its current position to the next adjacent track and begins to play. We measured this access time to be 2.0 seconds on this Pioneer unit. The time it takes the laser pickup to move from an inner track on a disc to an outer track on the same disc and begin playing is called "long access." For the PD-M6, that access time was 3.7 seconds.

Since this unit can also move from disc to disc, we made a third measurement to see how long it would take to switch from a track on one disc to a track on another disc mounted in the PD-M6 cartridge. The results: an amazing six seconds or less.

ERROR CORRECTION AND TRACKING

As has been true of most newer CD players, our Philips defects test disc was unable to trip up the excellent tracking and error correction of this Pioneer CD player. The PD-M6 changer had no trouble playing through the test disc's simulations of scratches (up to 900 microns in width), dust specks (up to 800 microns in diameter), and the fingerprint smudge that extends over two musical tracks.

This Pioneer CD changer's resistance to mild vibration and external shock was especially good. The player continued playing with no audible interruptions, skipping, or disc rejection while we repeatedly subjected it to less-than-gentle tapping along its top and side surfaces.

SUMMARY

The disc magazine is, as far as we are concerned, a good idea. First of all, it allows for the multiple-disc capabilities of this CD player. It also lets you leave the six (or fewer) CDs in the magazine, and safely store the magazine wherever you normally keep those "jewel cases" in which CDs are usually sold. One of the disc magazines takes up less than half the shelf width of six "jewel box" cases. It would have been nice if the magazine had some means for labeling the contents; perhaps that can be added by Pioneer or other companies at a later time.

For all the convenience of this magazine approach, we wonder if it will ever become the "standard," as Pioneer suggests. For one thing, extra magazines have a suggested price of $9.95 each. We realize that these magazines are much more than storage devices; they are mechanisms that must be made accurately in order to work inside the PD-M6. Nevertheless, it may be more than some people are willing to pay for a container that holds six discs.

Furthermore, as other test reports in this book demonstrate, this is but one approach to multiple-CD players. If every manufacturer designs players that handle different quantities of CDs and use different methods of installing those discs into the players, the likelihood that the industry can come up with any sort of standard is greatly diminished.

Still, if you like the idea of being able to install up to six discs in a convenient, protective magazine and play them sequentially or in any order you choose, it will be hard to resist this player. Needless to say, the discs do not touch each other even when the magazine is fully loaded.

Furthermore, an extremely clever mechanism accesses each disc for play, once the magazine is installed. Each disc never leaves its individual platform. Instead, the entire platform swings out and, since it has a large slot cut into its surface, the laser pickup is able to read the information stored beneath the disc's surface.

One thing that takes a bit of getting used to is the need to mount all of the discs into the magazine with the label side down. That's contrary to the way CDs are normally mounted in single-play machines that have front-loading drawers. Fortunately, there is no damage if you forget and load the discs label side up; they just won't play until you correct the situation. The price is reasonable and the sound quality is every bit as good as we've heard from similarly priced units that play one disc at a time. In other words, this is a "Best Buy."

MITSUBISHI DP-409R

Mitsubishi Electric Sales America, Inc.

MANUFACTURER'S SPECIFICATIONS:

Frequency Response: 5 Hz to 20 KHz, ±0.5 dB.
Signal-to-Noise Ratio: Greater than 98 dB.
Dynamic Range: Greater than 90 dB.
Total Harmonic Distortion: 0.003%.
Channel Separation: Greater than 98 dB.
Number of Programmable Events: 30.
Number of Discs Handled: 5.
Audio Output Level: 2.0 volts rms.
Dimensions: 16¾ Wide x 4⅛ High x 13⅜ inches Deep.
Approximate Retail Price: $500.
Approximate Low Price: $469.

The Mitsubishi CD Changer offers a total of 30 programming selections from any of up to 5 discs that can be loaded into its CD magazine. You will find that the Mitsubishi magazines fit perfectly inside a cabinet used for storing VHS videotapes. In fact, the slot on the front of this CD player closely resembles that on a front-loading videocassette recorder.

Besides manual playback of a CD from beginning to end, you can also easily program disc and track selections. Two "repeat play" modes are offered for playback of programmed selections or of all five CDs in the magazine. Track skip, fast reverse (audible) scan, and scanning of the next disc are also possible.

This player doesn't have a headphone jack or a control for adjusting output levels. We tested the DP-409R, which includes a wireless remote control that duplicates most of the functions found on the front panel. You can also buy this player without the remote-control module, as the model DP-309, for $450.

CONTROL PANEL LAYOUT

When you insert the magazine into the front-loading slot, a series of bars are lit up in the display, which is located to the right of the slot. These bars indicate which disc trays have been filled. (The trays and illuminated display bars are numbered 1 through 5.) The display also provides the usual data, such as track number, disc number, and elapsed time. While you are programming, the program number (1 through 30) is displayed in place of the elapsed time. To indicate if you are in the program mode or in a repeat-play mode, some words are illuminated.

To activate the audible music search and track advance or reverse functions, two sets of forward and reverse keys are furnished. A "Next" button lets you advance from one disc to the next, while numbered keys and program buttons are used to memorize up to 30 desired selections, in any order, from any of the five discs. When entering your choices for immediate play or for programming, you first press the button for the disc number you desire. Any subsequent numbers that you press will be entered automatically as the track number of that disc.

OUR LAB MEASUREMENTS

Frequency response for the Mitsubishi DP-409R varied less than one third of a decibel from 20 Hz to 20 KHz. Harmonic and intermodulation distortions measured impressively low. The signal-to-noise ratio was average for a good CD player, although not as good as claimed by Mitsubishi. Separation was 76 dB at mid-frequencies; this was quite a bit less than what we have come to expect from home CD players, but it was more than adequate for a good stereo effect.

Dynamic range was a very high 106 dB, while the access time for moving from one track to the next on a single disc was about 1.5 seconds. When the programming sequence called for the player to go from one track on a given disc to a track on a different disc, it took about 13 seconds, a rather long time.

ERROR CORRECTION AND TRACKING

As might be expected, the Mitsubishi CD changer handled our defects test disc as if it had no imperfections whatsoever, playing all the way through the scratch, dust speck, and fingerprint smudge simulations with no evidence of mistracking.

SUMMARY

The Mitsubishi changer was easy to use and very easy to load. While the Mitsubishi and the Pioneer units delivered satisfactory sound, the Mitsubishi DP-409R, in our opinion, was the winner as far as human engineering and ease of use were concerned.

The electronic circuitry of both of these changers is essentially that of earlier single-disc players. That is, neither of these two changer models employs some of the newer techniques, such as digital filtering and oversampling, which critical listeners believe yields marginally better sound quality. Nevertheless, the Mitsubishi DP-409R sounded as good to our listening panel as many of the highly rated single-disc players we recommended in Chapter 5.

The fact that this particular player uses a five-disc cartridge, while the Pioneer unit uses a six-disc holder and the Sony car and home changers both use a ten-disc cartridge, need not distress a potential user. After all, the cartridge is not something you are likely to want to move from one brand of player to another.

The important thing to consider is whether you will ever need to play more than five discs in a CD changer. If you don't think that's likely, the Mitsubishi rates well among the CD changers tested. If you feel that six discs played without interruption is what you will want, the Pioneer unit should be your choice. If a ten-disc changer is what you're after, choose the new Sony home CD changer.

Finally, if you want to load 50 discs or more into a CD player, we suggest you travel to Japan and buy one of those multiple-disc players that are sold for use in sing-along bars and night clubs.

GLOSSARY

Analog Filter

In any digital recording system it is necessary to filter out all frequencies above the highest audio frequency that you want to preserve or record. Most early CD players (and even some of today's lower cost units) employ so-called analog output filters.

While these devices do an effective job of filtering out unwanted supersonic frequencies, they also introduce time-delay errors between lower and higher frequencies of the musical program. Some keen listeners feel that these errors impair both the sound quality and the stereo definition or arrangement of instruments on the imaginary soundstage that the stereo music creates. Consequently, many newer CD players employ digital filtering to accomplish the same purpose. See Digital Filter.

Binary Code

A numbering system that uses only 0's and 1's to describe all possible numbers, much as is done by the numbers 0 through 9 that make up the decimal numbering system we use every day. The binary system lends itself to computer applications, as well as to the encoding of audio in the form of tiny "pits" inscribed beneath the surface of a Compact Disc. Binary number codes are used to describe the relative amplitude of the thousands of samples of an audio signal that are taken each second. In the standard CD format, each sample "number" consists of 16 0's and/or 1's; these combinations are known as 16-bit samples.

Glossary

Bit

Short for Binary digIT, a bit is a single "0" or "1" that is used in the binary numbering system employed in digital-audio and computer applications. An 8-bit binary number sample is called a byte. Thus, the 16-bit samples used to describe the instantaneous amplitude or loudness of an audio signal might be described as a 2-byte sample.

dB (Decibel)

A relative measure of sound or electrical signal intensity. We can speak of one sound as being, for instance, 3 dB louder than another sound, but the decibel itself has no absolute quantitative value. One decibel is approximately the smallest change in loudness that most people can perceive. It takes a change of ten decibels in loudness for us to perceive a sound as being twice as loud as another sound.

Digital Audio

The technique for converting continuous, or "analog," audio signals into a series of numeric values, and storing those values on some medium, such as a Compact Disc or magnetic tape. Then, during playback, the number codes are translated back into a replica of the original, continuous audio signals.

Digital Filter

A device for attenuating (reducing the amplitude of) all unwanted frequencies above 20,000 Hz (or 20 KHz, the upper limit of human hearing) in a CD player using digital, rather than analog, circuitry. Digital filtering is generally used with a technique called oversampling for marginally better sound reproduction. See Analog Filter and Oversampling.

Digital Master Tape

A professional studio tape recording that employs digital audio-recording techniques. Digitally mastered tapes were available long before CDs; many were used to master (act as an original recording for the creation of) so-called "digital LPs." In fact, such LPs were not digital at all; only the master tapes used to create these records were digital.

Conversely, not all CDs are made from digital master tapes. Often, a worthwhile performance that was originally stored on conventional, analog master tapes and made before digital tape recording was possible will be used to create a Compact Disc. There is nothing wrong with this practice, since the quality of those analog master tapes may still be better than the quality of even the best LP. By transferring the music to a CD, full advantage can be taken of the dynamic range and low distortion of a properly recorded analog master tape.

Dithering

A technique for adding a small amount of random noise to a digital recording. Surprisingly, this technique can actually increase the ultimate dynamic range of a CD, rather than decrease it. Dithering enables a listener to hear extremely soft sounds that might otherwise be lost because of the digital recording and playback processes.

Dynamic Range

The difference between the softest and loudest sounds that can be stored in a recording or that can be reproduced by an audio system. Compact Discs offer a potential dynamic range of 96 decibels or more. Since live music hardly ever exceeds 70 or 75 dB in dynamic range, this means that even the softest sounds stored on a CD are 20 to 25 dB below the residual noise level of the disc itself. It is for this reason that noise on a CD is inaudible. It's not that the noise doesn't exist; it's just too soft to be heard relative to the levels we use when listening to the music on the disc.

Error Correction

In any digital recording system, if data can't be read by the pickup device (in the case of a CD player, the laser pickup), it could result in gross errors in sound reproduction. In the CD format, a great deal of redundant information is encoded, so that if the laser fails to read data the first time, it can retrieve that data later on. Data is also staggered, so that a scratch on a CD, for example, would not result in the loss of many sequential samples.

The CD's error correction is so sophisticated that as many as 4,000 digital samples in a row can be missing or overlooked by the pickup, and the system will still correct the missing data perfectly.

Error Detection

Before error correction can take place, the CD player's electronics must detect the fact that an error (such as incorrectly read or missing data) has occurred. In newer CD players, the speed of error detection has been increased so that error correction can occur more swiftly and effectively.

Frequency Response

In an ideal recording, all of the tones, or frequency content, of the music should be stored and reproduced at exactly the same relative amplitude, or loudness, as they were played in the original performance. In order for this to take place, the reproducing device—in this case, the CD player—must uniformly reproduce all frequencies that fall in the range of human hearing. Such uniform response is said to be "flat response," and any deviation from perfect flatness, or uniformity, is noted in decibels.

Harmonic Distortion

Also called total harmonic distortion, or THD. The sum of all unwanted audio signals that are harmonically related to (multiples of) the desired tone (frequency) being reproduced by the audio component, but that were not part of the original tonal makeup of the music itself.

Harmonic distortion can be generated in many ways by electronic audio components. CD players generate far less distortion than do other components, such as amplifiers, preamplifiers, loudspeakers, and the like. Most people cannot detect harmonic distortion levels below 1% or so. A CD player might produce a mere 0.005% of harmonic distortion when reproducing a sound at its maximum recording level. CD player distortion tends to rise somewhat at lower recorded levels of sound, but the distortion is generally still too low to be detected by human hearing.

IM Distortion

IM, or intermodulation, distortion is another form of unwanted, electronically generated distortion. IM distortion arises when two or more signals at different frequencies create either sum or difference signals that were not part of the original music. For example, if two instruments in an orchestra produce frequencies of 9,000 Hz and 10,000 Hz, additional frequencies of 1,000 Hz (the difference) and 19,000 Hz (the sum) might be generated in small amounts. As is true of harmonic distortion, CD players produce virtually inaudible amounts of IM distortion.

Index Numbers

Some Compact Discs, in addition to being divided into "tracks," are further subdivided with index numbers. A movement of a symphony, for instance, might be given a track number on a CD. This movement may have two, three, or even more musical melodies or themes, each of which may be assigned an index number.

The purpose of index numbers is to allow the listener to access specific points within a track more easily. However, not all CD players can access index numbers and, conversely, not all CDs are encoded with index numbers. There's usually no point in assigning index numbers to a "pop" or "rock" disc that has only short selections recorded on it, each of which is already assigned a separate track number.

Interpolation

If the laser pickup of a CD player fails to read a series of samples that is too long for total error correction, the CD system may "fill in" what it surmises to be the missing samples. It does this by looking at the samples that came before the absence of data occurred, and then estimating the missing values based on the preceding, known data. This process of filling in the missing values by analyzing the data that preceded it is known as interpolation.

While this technique is not as accurate as true error correction, it does prevent audible interruptions in the music. If missing data is even more extensive, the CD player will ultimately go silent for a fraction of a second, or more, until the laser pickup is able to resume reading the data.

Laser Pickup

A movable assembly, or mechanism, that is suspended above or below the CD, but not in actual physical contact with it. The assembly contains a low-power laser whose light beam is reflected from below the surface of the CD. Changes in the disc's reflectivity, or reflectance, which are caused by the presence or absence of etched "pits," are sensed by a photocell (a component whose electrical properties are modified by the action of light). The photocell then translates these variations in the disc's reflectivity back into electrical signals that correspond to the digital number codes. These codes are ultimately translated back into an analog musical signal.

Linear Motor

A magnetically driven motor used to move the laser pickup across the surface of a Compact Disc. Because linear motors do not employ gears or rotating parts, they can move very rapidly along a guide rail. This enables CD players that use these motors to access any point on a disc in one second or less.

Oversampling

It has been found that by doubling or quadrupling the sample reading rate in a CD player, somewhat better sound reproduction can be obtained. Thus, many CD players use an internal sampling rate of 88,200 Hz, rather than 44,100 Hz. The number of samples encoded in the disc itself is still 44,100 for every second of recorded music; this is the standard sampling rate. You can think of oversampling as if the CD player is "reading" each sample twice. See Sampling Rate.

Programming

The act of loading instructions into the CD player's memory for execution at a later time. The complexity of programming offered by different CD players varies considerably. For example, some CD players permit only a few instructions to be programmed into memory, while others may accept as many as 99 individual instructions, which consist of tracks and index points to be played, as well as other pertinent information.

Glossary

Repeat Play

A feature in many CD players whereby the machine can be instructed to continually play either an entire CD or parts of a disc that have been programmed into memory. Many CD players also have a feature known as A-to-B repeat, in which a phrase or portion of music, selected by the listener, will be played repeatedly until this function is canceled.

Sampling Rate

In any digital recording system, the musical waveform (the graphical representation that shows the sound's amplitude in relation to its frequency) must be looked at, or sampled, so that we can digitize it (convert into 1's and 0's) so it can be processed by the computer chips in CD players. The sampling rate is the number of digital samples taken each second in a digital audio recording and playback system. In CDs, the sampling rate is set at 44,100 samples per second.

Signal-to-Noise Ratio

The difference, measured in decibels, between the loudest portion of a musical program and any residual background noise found on the recording medium (in this case, a CD). The higher the signal-to-noise (S/N) ratio, the better. A conventional analog LP record is usually capable of a signal-to-noise ratio of not much more than 60 or 65 dB. By contrast, a CD player and the discs themselves will normally exhibit signal-to-noise ratios of 90 dB or better.

Tracks

The defined and identifiable sections or selections recorded on a Compact Disc. While there are no actual grooves on the surface of a CD, the recorded material is nevertheless divided into tracks that can be accessed by their assigned numbers. Thus, a "pop" or "rock" CD might have ten different songs on it, each of which will have been assigned a track number, from 1 to 10.

On some CD players, you can access any track number directly by entering the track number on a numeric keypad. Other CD players may require you to advance sequentially, from one track to the next, as track numbers are shown on a front-panel display.

Wow-and-Flutter

A wavering of pitch often produced when playing analog records or tapes. Wow-and-flutter results from inconsistencies in the speed of rotation of a record turntable or from inconsistencies in the speed at which tape travels in a tape recorder. In the case of a CD player, there is no significant wow-and-flutter.

Although CDs also rotate on a form of turntable, the data that is read from the discs by the laser pickup is stored briefly in an electronic ''buffer'' memory. The data is then released in a completely uniform manner, governed not by the erratic rotation of the turntable, but by the precise timing of a quartz-crystal "clock" that sets the 44,100 sampling rate (or multiples thereof). The data is then translated back into analog signals.

DIRECTORY OF MANUFACTURERS

Akai America, Ltd.
800 W. Artesia Blvd.
Compton, CA 90220

**Bang & Olufsen of
America, Inc.**
1150 Feehanville Dr.
Mt. Prospect, IL 60056

Carver Corp.
P.O. Box 1237
Lynnwood, WA 98046

dbx, Inc.
Consumer Products
Div.
P.O. Box 100C
Newton, MA 02195

Denon America, Inc.
27 Law Dr.
Fairfield, NJ 07006

**Mitsubishi Electric
Sales America, Inc.**
P.O. Box 6007
Cypress, CA 90630-0007

**N.A.P. Consumer
Electronics Corp.**
P.O. Box 6950
Knoxville, TN 37914

**Pioneer Electronics
(USA) Inc.**
P.O. Box 1720
Long Beach, CA 90801

Shure Brothers Inc.
222 Hartrey Ave.
Evanston, IL
60202-3696

**Sony Corp. of
America**
Sony Dr.
Park Ridge, NJ 07656

**Studer Revox
America, Inc.**
Revox Div.
1425 Elm Hill Pike
Nashville, TN 37210

Technics
Consumer Affairs Dept.
Panasonic Co.
One Panasonic Way
Secaucus, NJ 07094

Toshiba America, Inc.
82 Totowa Rd.
Wayne, NJ 07470

**Yamaha Electronics
Corp., USA**
6660 Orangethorpe Ave.
Buena Park, CA 90620